I0606092

Beyoncé

Icon of our times

her life. her music. her style.

Carolyn McHugh

First published in the UK 2025 by Sona Books an imprint of Danann Publishing Ltd.

CAT NO: SON0612

Photography courtesy of

Getty images:

Kevin Mazur
Houston Chronicle/
Hearst Newspapers
L. Cohen
Steve Grayson
R. Diamond
Christopher Polk
Paul Hawthorne
Stuart C. Wilson/Stringer
Matt Winkelmeyer
MTV/MTV1415
CBS Photo Archive
Jim Spellman
Jason Merritt

Miguel J. Rodriguez Carrillo
Michael Blackshire
James Devaney
Gregg DeGuire
Gareth Cattermole
Lars Niki
Alo Ceballos
Julian Dakdouk/Parkwood Media
Kevin Winter/BET
MediaNews Group/Bay Area News
Dan MacMedan
Jamie McCarthy
Kevork Djansezian
Larry Busacca

Samir Hussein
Marc Piasecki
Patrick McMullan
Jim Smeal
Allen Berezovsky
E. Charbonneau
Evan Agostini
Bob Riha Jr
Paul McConnell
Scott Gries
Tim Mosenfelder
Raymond Boyd
Vinnie Zuffante
New York Daily News Archi

Other images Alamy, Wiki Commons

Cover design Darren Grice at Ctrl-d
Book design Alex Young at Cre8ive
Proof reader Cameron Thurlow
Editor Mathilde Pineau-Valencienne

Made in Dubai.

ISBN: 978-1-917259-00-2

Contents

Beyoncé:

The Cultural Icon

Introduction

Global sensation Beyoncé is a cultural icon whose influence reaches far beyond music. A singer, songwriter, dancer, actress, producer, business mogul, philanthropist and activist, she's a one-of-a-kind artist whose work perfectly captures the essence of modern times and has assured her of a place in the pantheon of all-time greatest Black female artists.

From humble beginnings in Houston, Texas, USA, where she grew up as Beyoncé Giselle Knowles, she's had a meteoric rise to take the throne as the international queen of pop and R&B. Beyoncé's journey is one of unparalleled talent, relentless determination, and visionary artistry.

Known as Queen Bey, she now reigns among the best-selling solo artists of all time with record sales topping 200 million worldwide and counting. And that's not to mention the 60 million records she sold as part of Destiny's Child, one of the best-selling female groups of all time, and where her career took off in the late 1990s.

This biography charts the path taken by a young girl with big dreams, to become a groundbreaking star who has redefined the boundaries of music, business and culture across multiple genres of music and visual albums, fashion and dance. All the while she has continually reinvented herself, breaking barriers and setting trends in an ever-changing industry and sparking vital conversations on race, feminism, and identity.

After 35 years in the music industry, eight solo studio albums, and 32 Grammy Award wins, Beyoncé now enjoys the single-name fame that very few artists achieve.

Recognised as the world's greatest living entertainer by *Rolling Stone* magazine in 2022, she is one of the most influential figures of our time, with upwards of 316 million followers on Instagram alone.

Destiny's Child's star on the Hollywood Walk of Fame

Beyoncé Knowles at age 19, photographed in Houston, Texas, 2 November 2001

This is the story of how she became not just a musical superstar, but a symbol of empowerment, creativity, and cultural change. Can you handle it?

Beyoncé:

Chapter 1

Early Life in Houston

Beyoncé's early life in Houston laid the foundation for the extraordinary career that would follow.

Born Beyoncé Giselle Knowles on 4 September, 1981, she was the first child of Mathew and Tina Knowles who had married in 1979. Her childhood in Houston, Texas, surrounded by the sounds of gospel and the influence of her parents, shaped the artist and the woman she would become.

Ambition, creativity, and hard work were woven into the very fabric of her family's identity. Her father, Mathew Knowles, born in Gadsden, Alabama, was a driven man who had worked his way up from modest beginnings to become a successful sales executive at Xerox. His work ethic, tenacity, and business acumen would later play a crucial role in Beyoncé's career, guiding her through the often treacherous waters of the music industry. But beyond his professional success, Mathew was a man with big dreams for his family in general and his eldest daughter in particular.

His wife, Beyoncé's mother, Celestine Ann 'Tina' Knowles (née Beyincé), was equally formidable. A Louisiana native with Creole roots, Tina was a talented fashion designer and hairdresser who owned a successful salon in Houston, specialising in African American styling.

This Creole heritage, a blend of African, Native American, and French influences, gave Beyoncé a rich cultural background that would later manifest in her music, fashion, and public persona. Tina's artistic sensibilities and eye for style would become integral to the visual aspects of Beyoncé's career, from her stage costumes to her music videos.

The Knowles family was close-knit, with strong values centred around faith, hard work, and perseverance. Beyoncé's parents believed that anything was possible with enough effort, dedication and determination, and instilled that in her and her younger sister, Solange, who was born 24 June 1986. Mathew and Tina's relationship was one

Family Christmas traditions: Beyoncé and Solange Knowles, 23 October, 1990

Tina Knowles in 2010

Tina was a talented **fashion designer** and hairdresser

of mutual respect and collaboration, and their combined influence created an environment that nurtured creativity and ambition.

Both Tina and Mathew were glamorous figures who loved music and had dabbled in the industry when they were younger – Tina performing in a group called The Beltones, and Mathew promoting bands during his time at Fish University in Nashville.

The Knowles family lived in a modest home in the middle-class neighbourhood of Third Ward, Houston. They were comfortably off and Beyoncé's early years were marked by the typical experiences of a middle-class upbringing, yet there were already signs that she was destined for something extraordinary. The city of Houston, with its melting pot of cultures and musical influences, provided a rich backdrop for her formative years. Houston was a city rich in cultural diversity where the vibrant music scene, including sounds of gospel, blues, jazz, and hip-hop, all blended seamlessly, creating a fertile ground for a young artist with an ear for music.

Although Beyoncé was generally a quiet and shy child, this reserve melted away when it came to music. She was dancing as soon as she took her first steps and her parents noticed her natural inclination towards performing as she sang around the house, her voice carrying a purity and strength beyond her years. Her love for music was evident, and recognising this, her parents provided her with as many opportunities as possible to explore and develop her talents.

One such opportunity came at the St John's United Methodist Church where the Knowles family worshipped regularly. Beyoncé was captivated by the powerful voices of the gospel choir whose raw emotion and spiritual depth resonated deeply with her, laying the foundation for the soulful elements that would later define her sound.

Beyoncé with her younger sister in support of Solange's debut album, 17 March, 2002

NY
MICHAEL JACKSON'S
THRILLER

When she sang, she found her voice – literally and figuratively. Singing became a way for her to express herself and connect with the world around her. For all her talents and stage presence, off stage Beyoncé could be shy and unsure of herself which made school a challenge for her.

But school was also another chance to train and her musical talents were well developed at St. Mary's Montessori School in Houston. In addition to singing, Beyoncé developed a love for dancing, which would become a key element of her performances. She had taken dance classes since she was seven and her natural rhythm and ability to learn routines with ease was immediately evident to her dance teacher, Darlette Johnson.

Darlette was the first to truly recognise the depth of her talent, impressed by Beyoncé's ability to hit every note perfectly while maintaining her dance moves. Trained in various dance styles, including jazz, ballet, and hip-hop, it was in the fusion of these styles that Beyoncé truly excelled. Her dance routines were characterised by their precision, energy, and creativity – qualities that would later become hallmarks of her performances.

It was during a school talent show that Beyoncé's potential as a performer became apparent to a larger audience. Her rendition of John Lennon's masterpiece *Imagine* was met with a standing ovation, and it became clear that this young

Beyoncé Knowles and her parents Tina and Mathew Knowles at the MGM Grand Garden Arena in Las Vegas, Nevada, 22 May, 2003

girl was destined for the stage – her voice was powerful, her stage presence magnetic, and her determination unmatched.

Seeing that Beyoncé's talent could be something more than just a hobby, Mathew and Tina decided to invest in their daughter's future, enrolling her in more music and dance lessons and encouraging her to participate in local talent shows. These early experiences not only honed her skills but also built her confidence as a performer. Winning talent shows became a regular occurrence for Beyoncé, and with each victory, as her 30-plus trophies piled up, so her desire to pursue a career in music grew stronger.

Happy times at Parkwood, Houston

The Knowles family moved to a large house in Parkwood Drive in the Third Ward of Houston during the mid-80s. It was a happy home, with lots of rooms and even a small stage in the back garden where Beyoncé and Solange would 'perform' as they played.

Such lovely memories lay behind Beyoncé's later decision to name her management company Parkwood. In a further nod to her background, Beyoncé's cousin Angie, to whom she was close, eventually became vice president of operations at the 400-strong Parkwood enterprise.

Beyoncé Knowles and Kelly Rowland of Destiny's Child perform at The Shark Bar in Chicago, Illinois in October 1997

In 1988, aged just seven, Beyoncé won her first national competition, the Baby Junior category of the contest run by the People's Family Workshop to promote the arts. She was invited to return the following year as a guest performer and as she sang *Home*, from the musical *The Wiz*, it was evident to all how far she had come during that year. She was polished, confident and, more importantly, pitch perfect as she performed the tricky song alongside step-perfect choreography.

She had undoubtedly been helped by the extra performing classes her parents could afford, including private one-to-one singing lessons with opera tenor David Lee Brewer.

In 1990, when she was aged nine, Beyoncé's life took a pivotal turn. She joined the 4th grade at Parker Elementary School in Houston, which was renowned for its musical curriculum. It was here that she got the chance to audition for an all-girls entertainment group being formed by a local producer. The group, initially called Girl's Tyme, was composed of other young Houston performers with dreams of stardom and included Beyoncé's friend and classmate LaTavia Roberson.

The other members at the start were sisters (and cousins of LaTavia) Nikki and Nina Taylor along with fifth member Ashley Támar Davis. A few months later the band's manager Andretta Tillman added a sixth girl to the lineup – Kelly Rowland, who would become one of Beyoncé's closest friends and collaborators.

Kelly was already a friend of LaTavia, so along with Beyoncé, this trio became inseparable on and off stage. Aged 11, Kelly eventually moved in with the Knowles family in an arrangement which suited both girls. As best friends they were happy to spend even more time with each other and be able to rehearse as much as they liked. Kelly still saw plenty of her own mother, who as a single parent, was now able to take work as a live in nanny.

As Beyoncé recalled in an interview with Blender magazine, she and Kelly were 'sleeping in the same bed... singing all day and loving every minute of it'.

Beyoncé's powerful voice and range, combined with a charismatic stage presence made her the standout member of the group, and she quickly became the lead singer. She always had a 'mama' vibe – first to her little sister Solange and later to the other members of the group.

Girl's Tyme was the precursor to what would later become Destiny's Child, marking the beginning of Beyoncé's journey into the world of professional music.

However, the path to success was not without its obstacles. Girl's Tyme faced numerous challenges in their early days, including lineup changes and struggles to find their identity as a group. Despite these setbacks, Beyoncé's passion for music never wavered. She spent countless hours practicing with the group, working on her vocal technique, and studying the performances of established artists. Her dedication was matched by her parents, who were equally committed to helping her achieve her dreams.

Slowly Girl's Tyme began to get noticed and in 1992, an R&B producer who came to see one of their gigs advised them to enter America's biggest TV talent show of the time, called Star Search.

It was their first major opportunity and everyone was confident it would give them their break, with the girls hoping to become as famous and successful as previous contestants including Justin Timberlake and Britney Spears. But it was not to be. The group, introduced as 'hip hop rappers', came second – not a bad

Destiny's Child in the studio in southwest Houston, 17 July, 1997. (L-R) LaTavia Roberson, Beyoncé Knowles, LeToya Luckett, Kelly Rowland

achievement at all, but to them missing out on the top spot was a crushing blow, dashing their dreams of a recording contract and leaving them in tears.

It could have ended their journey. But instead the experience prompted a rethink and Beyoncé's father Mathew decide to become more involved, persuading their manager Andretta to let him co-manage. With his background in sales and marketing, Mathew approached Beyoncé's career with a business-minded focus. He understood the importance of building a brand and navigating the complexities of the music industry and was relentless in his efforts to get Beyoncé and Girls Tyme noticed. His approach was hands-on – he managed every aspect of the group's career, from choreography to wardrobe. Mathew's ambitious vision was clear: he wanted Beyoncé, and what he saw as 'her' group, to become superstars, and he was willing to do whatever it took to make that happen.

So instead of letting the defeat derail them, Mathew used the experience as a lesson in resilience. Under his guidance, the group began rehearsing even more rigorously. The girls, including new member LeToya Luckett, trained like athletes, literally running as they sang to build up stamina, honing their vocals, perfecting choreography, and learning the intricacies of the music business. Despite their youth, the members of Girl's Tyme were taught to approach their craft with professionalism.

Mathew and Tina were undoubtedly the architects of Beyoncé's early career and instrumental in shaping the artist and the woman she would become. Each brought unique strengths to the table, creating a support system that was both nurturing and strategic.

While Mathew handled the business side of things, Tina was the creative force behind Beyoncé's image. As a talented fashion designer and stylist, Tina played a crucial role in shaping the visual aspects of her daughter's career. She designed the group's costumes, creating looks that were both stylish and age-appropriate.

The group continued to work hard, and over time, its lineup began to change. Members came and went, and by the mid-1990s, the group had been pared down to four core members: Beyoncé, Kelly Rowland, LaTavia Roberson, and LeToya Luckett.

With this more focused lineup, the group began to build up their performance CV by supporting some more established R&B acts, eventually bagging a few record company auditions and being signed by the Elektra label. The early days went well and the girls moved to Atlanta to begin work on an album. But then the label's executives reconsidered, coming to believe that the group was too young, and decided to drop them, which was another huge blow.

Describing it as 'a defining moment', Mathew was rocked by Elektra's decision. So much so that in an 'all or nothing' gamble, he gave up his job with Xerox to devote his energies to managing the group full-time. Andretta agreed to move aside as she was increasingly unwell after being diagnosed with the auto-immune disease lupus.

Now in full charge, Mathew decided that the group needed a rebrand. Girl's Tyme was renamed as Destiny's Child... you might have heard of them...

Destiny's Child in the studio in southwest Houston, 17 July, 1997.

Beyoncé:

The Destiny's Child Era

Chapter 2

The name Destiny's Child was inspired by a passage from the Bible's Book of Isaiah, reflecting the group's spiritual roots and sense of purpose.

Purpose was definitely not lacking. Beyoncé, Kelly, LaTavia and LeToya were excited by their new, more 'grown up' name and image, while Mathew was excited to make his mark, even taking a course in artistic management to shore up his new role.

His decision to leave his well-paying job at Xerox to manage Beyoncé and the band was a testament to his belief in their potential. To his credit, he wanted to give his daughter every opportunity to succeed, and to guide her through auditions, negotiations, and the many challenges that came with pursuing a career in music. But it was a risky move which put the whole family under financial strain.

As Beyoncé's career had begun to take off, the Knowles family faced the challenge of balancing their personal lives with the demands of the music industry. The pressures of fame and success were intense, but Mathew and Tina worked hard to ensure that Beyoncé and her sister Solange had as normal a home life as possible. They emphasised the importance of education, discipline, and maintaining strong family bonds, values that would remain with Beyoncé throughout her life.

But despite their best efforts, the family's pursuit of Beyoncé's dreams was not without sacrifices. The financial strain of supporting her career ambitions led to challenges at home, and the Knowles's had to downsize and move to a much smaller flat and generally scale back their lifestyle.

The pressure took a toll on Mathew and Tina's marriage and they even briefly separated. However, their unwavering belief in Beyoncé's potential kept them going. They were determined to see their daughter succeed, even though it meant big personal sacrifices.

Destiny's Child promotional visit in Chicago, April 1998

All the blood, sweat and toil paid off when Destiny's Child got their breakthrough in 1997.

Musician D'Wayne Wiggins heard one of their demo tapes and signed the group to his Grass Roots Entertainment company, through which they got the opportunity to try out for Columbia Records in New York.

Their audition had to be a cappella but this is where their many years of performance and rehearsal paid off. Everything went well and they sang their audition pieces – their own compositions of *Are You Ready* and *Ain't No Sunshine* by Bill Withers – perfectly. Columbia signed them.

Preparations for their self-titled debut album went well – the band's enthusiasm and work ethic was matched by a strong list of songs written over the years of waiting.

Released in 1998, the album's tracks featured a blend of R&B, hip-hop, and pop that suited the group's vocal harmonies and youthful energy. It included the single *No, No, No*, which became their first major hit, with a remixed version featuring Wyclef Jean. The success of this *No, No, No Part 2* remix gave Destiny's Child their first taste of fame, as it reached the top ten on the Billboard Hot 100, earning them a gold certification, and reached #5 in the UK singles chart.

Destiny's Child ▶

Debut album released 17 February 1998

Track listing

Second Nature
No, No, No Part 2 (Ft. Wyclef Jean)
With Me Part I (Ft. Jermaine Dupri)
Tell Me
Bridges
No, No, No Part 1
With Me Part II (Ft. Master P)
Show Me the Way
Killing Time
Illusion (Ft. Wyclef Jean & Pras)
Birthday
Sail On
My Time Has Come

The album was a middling success, debuting at #69, peaking at #67, and spending 26 weeks on the US Billboard 200 albums chart altogether. It earned first gold then platinum RIAA certification. In the UK the album made #45 on the UK albums chart and cracked the Top 30 in Canada and the Netherlands.

Despite this breakthrough, the road ahead was still uncertain. The music industry was fickle, and Destiny's Child needed to prove that they weren't just a one-hit wonder. Their second album, *The Writing's on the Wall* (1999), would become the make-or-break moment for the group.

In the end, *The Writing's on the Wall* made them. It was a game-changer, marking their evolution from a gospel-rooted R&B girl group to masters of progressive pop and soul, with fully developed production and arrangements.

The hit singles from it, including *Bills, Bills, Bills, Bug a Boo, Jumpin', Jumpin',* and *Say My Name,* cemented their place in the music industry. Each of these songs not only topped charts, but also became anthems of female freedom.

Bills, Bills, Bills became Destiny's Child's first #1 hit on the Billboard Hot 100, while their second #1, *Say My Name,* would go on to become one of the group's most celebrated songs, earning them two Grammy Awards. The lyrics, dealing with themes of independence, self-respect, and relationship dynamics, struck a chord with audiences and established Destiny's Child as more than just a pop group – they were a voice for a generation of young women navigating life and love.

Destiny's Child attend the 1998 Soul Train Music Awards in Los Angeles, California, 27 February, 1998

Selling 13 million copies worldwide, *The Writing's on the Wall* is one of the best-selling R&B albums of all time. Beyoncé was key to this latest music, writing and co-producing 17 of the album's tracks, working with collaborators including Missy Elliott, Timbaland and Kevin 'She'kspere' Briggs. She also used her staccato rap singing style for the first time – a vocal cadence technique which has since become hugely popular and mimicked by other major urban and pop artists.

The Writing's on the Wall ▸

Second album, released 14 July 1999

Track listing

Intro (The Writing's on the Wall)
So Good
Bills, Bills, Bills
Confessions (Ft. Missy Elliott)
Bug a Boo
Temptation
Now That She's Gone
Where'd You Go
Hey Ladies
If You Leave (Ft. Next)
Jumpin', Jumpin'
Say My Name
She Can't Love You
Stay
Sweet Sixteen
Outro (Amazing Grace)

At last the group was enjoying the recognition and rewards for which Beyoncé and her family had worked so hard. However, the demands of fame and the pressures of the music industry began to strain the group's dynamics. The relationships within the group, which had once been based on friendship and shared dreams, were now complicated by business and intense public scrutiny. This tension came to a head in early 2000 when LaTavia Roberson and LeToya Luckett were replaced by Michelle Williams, a former backing singer, and Farrah Franklin

The new look Destiny's Child three piece lineup make a glittering arrival at the Source Hip Hop Music Awards in 2000

who had danced in the group's video for *Bills Bills Bills*. The sudden lineup change shocked fans and created a media frenzy, with rumours of infighting and power struggles whizzing around.

LaTavia and LeToya, who had been with the group since its early days, were reportedly unhappy with the management and direction of the group, particularly Mathew Knowles' leadership. Their departure led to lawsuits and public disputes, which cast a shadow over the group's rise. For Beyoncé, this period was especially challenging. As the group's de facto leader, and Mathew's daughter, she found herself in the uncomfortable position of being seen as responsible for the shake-up. The media portrayed her as the 'queen bee' who had ousted her former friends, a narrative that was obviously as painful as it was potentially damaging.

The way Destiny's Child handled the public's perception of them was a defining aspect of this period. Beyoncé, in particular, faced the dual burden of leading the group while also managing the narrative around their lineup changes. Her poise and professionalism during interviews and public appearances helped to steady the group's image, even as rumours and criticisms swirled.

Farrah Franklin's tenure in the group was brief – she left after just five months in the group, citing stress and poor working conditions. This left Destiny's Child as a trio, comprising Beyoncé, Kelly, and Michelle. Despite the turmoil, the new lineup quickly gelled and continued to produce hits. The group's chemistry was undeniable, and they pushed ahead with renewed focus.

With their new lineup, the dynamics within Destiny's Child became more streamlined, with each member playing to her strengths. Beyoncé's role as the lead vocalist was clear, but Kelly and Michelle also began to shine in their own right. Kelly's soulful voice provided a rich counterpoint to Beyoncé's powerful delivery, while Michelle's gospel background added depth to their harmonies. This balance allowed Destiny's Child to explore a wider range of musical styles, from pop and R&B to gospel and hip-hop.

In 2001, Destiny's Child released *Survivor*, an album that would become their defining work. The title track was an anthem of resilience and empowerment, reflecting the group's journey through adversity. The album was a huge commercial success, debuting at #1 on the Billboard 200, topping the charts in 18 countries in total, earning the band global attention and further critical acclaim.

In a UK radio interview promoting the album, Beyoncé said that she would never have predicted such success but reminded listeners Destiny's Child had been going for five years, she herself having started working at the age of nine and first recording when she was 14. 'So it [the album's success] didn't happen fast and it didn't happen by coincidence,' she said. 'It happened because of hard work, and sacrifice, and God. This ain't no little kids' job, we employ hundreds and thousands of people...millions of people depend on us, so it's serious and we take it seriously, that's why we try to put positive messages in our songs and we try to be good role models'.

The group put in the hard yards of interviews and promotional appearances and by the end of the year *Survivor* had sold some three million copies. Tracks such as *Bootylicious* and *Independent Women Part I* solidified their status as strong models of female independence, encouraging their fans to stand strong in the face of adversity.

The album was a huge commercial success

Survivor ▲

Released 25 April 2001

Track listing

Independent Women Part 1
Survivor
Bootylicious
Nasty Girl
Fancy
Apple Pie á la Mode
Sexy Daddy
Independent Women Part 2
Happy Face
Emotion
Dangerously in Love
Brown Eyes
The Story of Beauty
Gospel Medley
Outro

By the early 2000s, Destiny's Child had established themselves as one of the most successful female groups in music history. Their influence extended far beyond their chart-topping hits; they had become cultural icons. Destiny's Child was not only a musical powerhouse but also a brand representing independence and resilience.

Musically, the group played a crucial role in shaping the sound of contemporary R&B and pop. They were at the forefront of a movement that blended traditional R&B with hip-hop elements, a style that would come to dominate the charts in the 2000s. Their ability to deliver catchy hooks, combined with their vocal prowess, set a new standard for girl groups. In particular Beyoncé's staccato rap vocal style was a defining feature of their work.

Destiny's Child also broke new ground with their music videos and live performances. Their visuals were bold and stylish, often incorporating high fashion and intricate choreography, elements which became hallmarks of their brand. Their performances were known for their energy and precision, with each member contributing to a dynamic stage presence that captivated audiences around the world.

Beyond their musical achievements, Destiny's Child had a profound impact on the representation of women in the music industry, challenging the traditional roles by taking control of their image and sound. This was particularly significant in a genre that had often relegated women to the roles of mere performers, rather than creators.

They were so successful that the girls felt secure enough to take a hiatus and began to explore solo opportunities. For Beyoncé, it was a chance to delve into her own musical influences, hone her songwriting skills, and develop a sound that was distinctly hers.

But she also found herself also in demand as an actress. The 9/11 terrorist attacks had forced Destiny's Child to reschedule their planned European tour that autumn, leaving a gap in the diary which enabled Beyoncé to take the lead role in the tv show 'Carmen: A Hip Hopera'. This was, as it sounds, an adaptation of the Bizet original, but with an African American twist. Her great reviews led to other opportunities including her first movie role as Foxxy Cleopatra in the successful 2002 spy comedy 'Austin Powers in Goldmember'. Echoing her positive reviews an impressed critic for the New York Times declared, 'Ms Knowles knows how to strut that strut'.

A second successful movie role came the following year in *The Fighting Temptations* with Cuba Gooding Jr. Beyoncé celebrated her 21st birthday during the shoot.

But her solo success truly peaked in 2003 when Beyoncé released her own well received studio album *Dangerously in Love*. The sleeve notes declared that the album came during a 'sojourn' from Destiny's Child. But in fact it was such a powerhouse album, on which Beyoncé had showcased her vocals and versatility as well as co-writing and co-producing almost all the tracks, that it signalled her eventual inevitable departure from the Texan supergroup.

During the band's two year hiatus Kelly and Michelle also explored solo opportunities. Kelly had a hit single *Dilemma* – a duet with rapper Nelly – in 2002, while Michelle was beginning a career in gospel music and theatre.

With everyone's solo career flourishing, maintaining the group became increasingly challenging and it was clear that Destiny's Child was all grown up and drawing to a close.

Destiny's Child in 2002

In 2004, the group reformed to release a final studio album, *Destiny Fulfilled*, which was seen as a celebration of their journey and legacy. The album featured hits like *Lose My Breath* and *Soldier* and was a great tribute to the growth and maturity of the group as artists.

Destiny Fulfilled ▸

Final album released November 2004

Track listing

Lose My Breath
Soldier (Ft. T.I, and Lil Wayne)
Cater 2 U
T-Shirt
Is She the Reason
Girl
Bad Habit
If
Free
Through with Love
Love

Due to an internet leak the album made an early and unexpected debut at #19 on the US Billboard 200 chart, before peaking at #2 in the US and #5 in the UK. It went on to sell over seven million copies and win triple platinum certification, as well as gaining five Grammy Award nominations.

Destiny's Child officially announced their disbandment in 2005, during their *Destiny Fulfilled... and Lovin' It* tour.

The announcement was presented as a mutual decision, with the members explaining, 'We have been working together as Destiny's Child since we were 9 and touring together since we were 14. After a lot of discussions and some deep soul searching, we realised that our current tour has given us the opportunity to leave Destiny's Child on a high note, united in our friendship and filled with overwhelming gratitude for our music, our fans, and each other.

'After all these wonderful years working together, we realised that now is the time to pursue our personal goals and solo efforts in earnest...No matter what happens, we will always love each other as friends and sisters and will always support each other as artists. We want to thank all of our fans for their incredible love and support and hope to see you all again as we continue fulfilling our destinies.'

They had achieved what they set out to do as a group, and it felt like a natural time to move on to new challenges. Their final performance took place on 10 September 2005, at the last show of their tour in Vancouver, Canada.

Destiny's Child perform part of the band's *Destiny Fulfilled... And Lovin' it* Tour in Oakland California on 3 September, 2005 just one week before their final performance

Destiny's Child: Tour triumphs

Destiny's Child embarked on three major tours during their career:

Say My Name Tour (2000)

This 32-date tour supported their second studio album, *The Writing's on the Wall and* primarily focused on North America.

Destiny's Child World Tour (2002)

This was their first major headlining tour, and supported their third studio album, *Survivor*. It took them across North America, Europe, Asia, and Africa for a total of 63 shows.

Destiny Fulfilled... and Lovin' It (2005)

This tour supported their final studio album, *Destiny Fulfilled*. It was also their farewell tour before disbanding. It included a total of 67 shows, taking the group around North America, and over to Europe, Asia, and Australia.

Destiny's Child with their Grammys backstage at the 43rd Annual Grammy Awards in 2001

Golden girls

Destiny's Child's journey from local Houston group to global superstars is a testament to their talent, hard work and resilience.

Their impressive list of achievements, which puts them among the all-time-great musical trios and most successful and influential girl groups ever, includes:

Sales of more than 60 million records

14 Grammy Award nominations (making them the most nominated girl group in Grammy history)

2 Grammy Award wins (Best R&B Performance by a Duo or Group with Vocals and Best R&B Song in 2001 for *Say My Name*)

Artist of the Year and Duo/Group of the Year at the 2001 Billboard Music Awards

Now a young woman, Beyoncé had begun to take on more responsibility for her career, learning the ins and outs of the music business from her father and developing her own artistic vision. Although her parents' influence remained strong, Beyoncé was starting to forge her own path. She was no longer just a talented child with a dream – she was an emerging artist with a clear sense of purpose and a burning desire to make her mark on the world.

Destiny's Child was the foundation upon which she would build an even more extraordinary solo career.

As a review on the BBC put it, 'There was only ever gonna be one winner in the Queen of Destiny's Child sweepstakes and her name is Beyoncé.' And so it proved to be...

Beyoncé:

Going solo – B'Day

Chapter 3

The idea of Beyoncé pursuing a solo career had been a topic of discussion even before Destiny's Child went on hiatus in 2001. Having already proven her vocal and performance abilities, the industry and fans alike were curious about what she could achieve on her own.

Beyoncé's decision to go solo was not just about pursuing personal fame; it was about creative control. She wanted to write, produce, and sing songs that reflected her life experiences, emotions, and aspirations. This control over her music would become a defining feature of her solo career, allowing her to push boundaries and experiment with different genres and themes.

Beyoncé's 2003 debut solo album, *Dangerously in Love*, had been pivotal in her career, marking her triumphant transition from the lead singer of Destiny's Child to a solo artist.

Critics also appreciated the album's diversity in musical styles, which spanned R&B, pop, hip-hop, and even a touch of reggae – an eclectic mix which was seen as a reflection of Beyoncé's versatility and ambition as a solo artist.

Critics viewed the lead single *Crazy in Love* as a defining moment in her career, calling it an 'instant classic', and a 'pop masterpiece'. The single gave Beyoncé her first solo #1 in the US and the UK. With the album *Dangerously in Love* making #1 at the same time, Beyoncé became the first woman to top both charts simultaneously in the US and the UK. *Crazy in Love* went on to top the US charts for eight consecutive weeks.

Beyoncé performing in 2003

Dangerously in Love ▶

Released June 2003

Track List

Crazy in Love (Ft. Jay-Z)
Naughty Girl
Baby Boy (Ft. Sean Paul)
Hip Hop Star (Ft. Big Boi & Sleepy Brown)
Be With You
Me, Myself and I
Yes
Signs (Ft. Missy Elliott)
Speechless
That's How You Like It (Ft. Jay-Z)
The Closer I Get to You (with Luther Vandross)
Dangerously in Love 2
Beyoncé Interlude
Gift From Virgo
Work It Out
'03 Bonnie & Clyde / Daddy

Greeted with huge critical acclaim and commercial success, the album made its debut at #1 on the Billboard 200 chart and sold over 300,000 copies in its first week. The album would go on to sell over 11 million copies worldwide, establishing Beyoncé as a formidable solo artist. It won her five Grammy Awards (from six nominations) at the 2004 ceremony – Best Contemporary R&B Album, Best Female R&B Vocal Performance (for *Dangerously in Love 2*) Best R&B performance by a Duo or Group with Vocals (for *The Closer I Get To You* with Luther Vandross), and Best R&B Song and Best Sung/Rap Collaboration (both with Jay-Z for *Crazy in Love*).

Dangerously in Love was a bold statement which blended R&B, hip-hop, soul, and pop, illustrating Beyoncé's versatility as an artist. The album's themes of love, strength, and independence resonated with a wide audience, and its production featured collaborations with some of the biggest names in music, including Jay-Z, Missy Elliott, and Sean Paul.

2004 was a hugely busy year for Beyoncé, and got off to a flying start when she achieved her longtime ambition to sing the American national anthem at the Super Bowl in February. Her acclaimed rendition of The Star Spangled Banner was watched by an estimated 130 million viewers in the US and a total of one billion people around the world.

Next the accolades kept coming as she won five out of the six Grammy nominations she had received for *Dangerously In Love*.

Also that month she picked up the prestigious UK Brit award for International Female Artist. It was one of her most successful months ever and underlined her arrival on the world stage.

But despite such stunning solo success, Beyoncé was back in the studio later that year to fulfil her commitment for a final album with Destiny's Child, followed by their farewell tour.

In between recording sessions she was keeping her acting career on the boil, with a role in The Pink Panther remake, starring comedian

Steve Martin. She also launched her own clothing label House of Deréon, named after her maternal grandmother Agnéz Deréon who had been a seamstress in Louisiana.

Having played Destiny Child's final ever show on 10 September 2005, Beyoncé could then begin her solo career proper.

She kicked off 2006 by going back in a movie studio for her role as Deena Jones in Dreamgirls, straight after which she started work on her second solo studio album, *B'Day*. This marked a significant moment in her career, confirming her as a dominant force in the music industry. She recorded all 10 tracks in just three weeks because she said that she wanted to lay them down while she was still channelling Deena, saying 'I was so inspired [by Deena] I wrote songs that were saying all the things I wish she would have said in the film'.

Beyonce sings the National Anthem to kick off the Super Bowl in 2004

Beyonce and Steve Martin at the World Premiere of *The Pink Panther* in 2006

The album, which was released on her 25th birthday, 4 September 2006, was met with critical acclaim – the few reservations that there were reflected the diverse perspectives on its musical and lyrical idiosyncrasies.

As on *Dangerously in Love* before it, one of the most universally praised aspects of the album was Beyoncé's vocal performance, with critics lauding her ability to convey emotion and power through her voice.

Her versatility was highlighted across a range of styles, from upbeat dance tracks to emotional ballads. The album's production, largely managed by a team of high-profile producers including Swizz Beatz, The Neptunes, and Rich Harrison, was also celebrated for its energetic and polished sound.

B'Day was also celebrated for its exploration of themes related to female independence. Songs like *Irreplaceable* and *Ring the Alarm* were noted for their strong, assertive messages. This album was the first where every song had an accompanying musical video – an approach which would be celebrated and much imitated in the future.

Damien Fahey chats with Beyoncé during her appearance on MTV's Total Request Live September 5, 2006 in New York City

B'Day (September 2006) ▲

Track listing

Standard Edition:

Déjà Vu (Ft. Jay-Z)
Get Me Bodied
Suga Mama
Upgrade U (Ft. Jay-Z)
Ring the Alarm
Kitty Kat
Freakum Dress
Green Light
Irreplaceable
Resentment

***Tracks added to Deluxe Edition (2007):**

Beautiful Liar (with Shakira)*
Welcome to Hollywood (Ft. Jay-Z)*
Flaws and All*
World Wide Woman*
Get Me Bodied (Extended Mix) *
Amor Gitano (with Alejandro Fernández) *(Spanish track)* *
Listen *(from the movie Dreamgirls)* *
Irreplaceable *(Spanish version)* *
Beautiful Liar *(Spanish version with Shakira)*

Additionally, the *B'Day Anthology Video Album* included music videos for nearly all tracks, further enhancing the album's impact and providing a visual representation of Beyoncé's artistic vision.

B'Day debuted at #1 on the Billboard 200, selling half a million copies in its first week on sale. In the UK it reached #3 and was also a Top Ten hit around Europe. It won the 2007 Grammy for Best Contemporary R&B album.

The lead single *Déjà Vu* was her second UK #1 and crowned *B'Day* as a triumph, underlining Beyoncé's ability to deliver a cohesive and dynamic project that resonated with a wide audience.

Then what really solidified her status as a global superstar was the 2007 Beyoncé Experience worldwide tour supporting the album. Including over 90 shows across North America, Europe, Asia, Africa, and Australia, the tour's positive reviews and high-profile performances contributed to her growing influence as one of the foremost figures in pop and R&B music. She had become, as track nine on her album put it, 'irreplaceable'.

She had become, as track nine on her album put it, 'irreplaceable'.

Beyoncé with her 2007 Grammy for Best Contemporary R&B album

Beyoncé performs on the opening night of her "B'day" world tour in Sydney, Australia, 21 April, 2007

Beyoncé:

Chapter 4

Love, Family, and Fame – The Beyoncé and Jay-Z Story

The love story of Beyoncé and Jay-Z is one of the most compelling in modern music. Their relationship, which has spanned over two decades, is a tale of love, partnership, family, and fame, woven together by their shared passion for music and their mutual respect for one another. Together, they have navigated the challenges of being in the spotlight while building an empire that transcends music, influencing culture, business, and social change.

Beyoncé first crossed paths with Shawn Corey Carter, known to the world as Jay-Z, in the late 1990s. Both were rising stars in the music industry, with Beyoncé making waves in Destiny's Child, and Jay-Z establishing himself as one of the most influential rappers and entrepreneurs in the hip-hop world.

Their initial meeting was purely professional, reportedly while both were on a flight to the MTV Spring Break Festival in Cancun, Mexico in 2000, but there was an undeniable chemistry between them. 'I was 18 when we first met, 19 when we first started dating,' Beyoncé once revealed. 'We were friends first for a year and a half before we went on any dates." she said.

Their romantic relationship began quietly, away from the prying eyes of the public. In an industry where celebrity relationships often become tabloid fodder, Beyoncé and Jay-Z were determined to keep their budding romance private. In 2002 they appeared together on the track *'03 Bonnie & Clyde*, a collaboration that hinted at their deepening bond. The song, which became a big hit, featured the duo as modern-day outlaws in love, a theme that resonated with fans and solidified their status as the power couple to end all power couples.

Their collaboration extended beyond their personal lives into their professional careers, where they consistently supported and inspired each other. This partnership was evident in their music, with Beyoncé appearing on Jay-Z's tracks and vice versa.

'Bonnie & Clyde' - Beyoncé and Jay-Z in 2002

Jay-Z appeared on Beyoncé's hit single, *Crazy in Love* and *That's How You Like It* from her 2003 debut album *Dangerously In Love* and made appearances on *Déjà Vu* and *Upgrade U* on her second album, *B'Day*. As their relationship grew, so did their influence. Beyoncé and Jay-Z understood that together, they were stronger – not just as a couple, but as a brand.

They eventually went public with a red carpet appearance together for the 2004 VMAs, after which her fame went to another level.

He was the first boyfriend that the public had known about and apparently from a different background, which fascinated the media. The relationship was game changing. As questions about the couple began to dominate interviews, Beyoncé began to do fewer of them, sliding under the radar as access to her began to dwindle.

In keeping with their low profile relationship, they were eventually married on 4 April 2008, in a small, private ceremony in Tribeca, New York City. Never officially announcing the wedding, Beyoncé only confirmed the event by eventually wearing her wedding ring – a Lorraine Schwartz design, reportedly worth US$5m. Their secret wedding was a reflection of their desire to keep their personal lives sacred, with only close friends and family in attendance. They chose the fourth of the month because of the number's special significance as both were born on the 4th, Beyoncé on 4 September and Jay-Z on 4 December. They even have matching 'IV' tattoos on their ring fingers.

Yet their relationship wasn't just about love; it was also about mutual respect. Beyoncé often credited Jay-Z with encouraging her to take control of her career, leading her to make bold decisions that shaped her trajectory as a solo artist. For his part, Jay-Z admired Beyoncé's work ethic and dedication, often referring to her as a driving force in his life. Together, they became a symbol of Black excellence, breaking barriers in an industry that had often marginalised Black artists.

As a married couple, Beyoncé and Jay-Z continued to dominate the music industry, but their focus began to shift towards starting a family. In 2011, Beyoncé announced her pregnancy during a performance at the MTV Video Music Awards, a moment that quickly became iconic.

On 7 January 2012, they welcomed their first child, a daughter named Blue Ivy Carter. The birth of Blue Ivy was a significant moment not just for the couple but also for their fans, who had followed their journey closely. Beyoncé and Jay-Z were overjoyed, and they made it clear that family was their top priority. Blue Ivy's arrival also marked the beginning of a new era for the couple, as they balanced parenthood with their careers. Blue Ivy became a big sister in June 2017 when Beyoncé gave birth to twins with Jay-Z, a daughter named Rumi and a son named Sir.

Glory for Blue Ivy

Just two days after Blue Ivy was born, her father Jay-Z released a song dedicated to her, called *Glory,* which was about his and Beyoncé's struggles to have children, including multiple miscarriages.

The end of the song included Blue Ivy's cries, for which she was credited as 'B.I.C.' (Blue Ivy Carter) earning her a chart entry as the youngest person in history to enter the Billboard chart when Glory made #74 on the Hot R&B/Hip-Hop Songs.

Then in 2021, when she was eight years (and 322 days) old, Blue Ivy picked up the Guinness World Record for the youngest individually credited person to win a Grammy when her work with Beyoncé and her songwriting team on *Brown Skin Girl* from the 2019 soundtrack album *The Lion King: The Gift*, won the Best Music Video category. The same song won the BET Her Award, similarly making Blue Ivy the youngest winner of all time.

As she grew up Blue showed a lot of interest in the arts generally and in performing too, appearing on stage during her mother's Renaissance tour, when she was aged just 12.

In a 2024 interview with GQ magazine Beyoncé praised Blue Ivy's talents, describing her as a '...fantastic editor, painter, and actress [who has] been creating characters since she was three. She's a natural, but I did not want Blue on stage. Blue wanted it for herself. She took it seriously and she earned it...and most importantly, she had fun! We all watched her grow more and more every night before our eyes.'

Blue Ivy's made her feature film debut in the 2024 release *Mufasa: The Lion King* – serving as a prequel and sequel based around the 2019 remake of the original *Lion King* movie. She played Kiara, the granddaughter of Mufasa's friend Rafiki.

Blue Ivy Carter in 2020

Later in 2012 the family moved into a large and luxurious US$88 million home in Bel Air, Los Angeles.

Life seemed perfect for the Carter family, but then came challenges. Rumours that the marriage was having problems around Jay-Z's infidelity, were fuelled by the infamous elevator incident in May 2014 involving Beyoncé's sister, Solange.

The incident quickly became a major media sensation. In response, the family issued a joint statement saying that they had resolved the matter privately and asking for privacy. The statement mentioned that they had been working through some issues and that the incident was an isolated one.

Nevertheless, the incident fuelled speculation with many beginning to wonder if their marriage was in trouble. But despite the public scrutiny, Beyoncé, Jay-Z, and Solange have since maintained a united front, with their relationship appearing to be repaired and strong.

However, Beyoncé addressed the rumours head-on in her 2016 album *Lemonade*. The album was a deeply personal exploration of love, betrayal, forgiveness, and redemption. Through her music, Beyoncé told the story of a woman scorned but also of a woman willing to fight for her marriage. *Lemonade* was critically acclaimed and resonated with many women who had faced similar struggles.

Jay-Z responded with his own album, *4:44*, released in 2017. The album was an apology, a reflection on his mistakes, and a testament to his commitment to making amends. Through songs like *4:44* and *Family Feud*, Jay-Z opened up about his shortcomings and the impact they had on his marriage. Together, the albums represented a public acknowledgment of their challenges and a reaffirmation of their love and commitment to each other, with their willingness to be vulnerable and honest about their struggles seemingly strengthening their bond.

Beyond their music, Beyoncé and Jay-Z have built an empire spanning multiple industries. They have become influential figures in fashion, with Beyoncé's Ivy Park line and Jay-Z's Rocawear brand. They've also made significant contributions to social justice, using their platforms to advocate for change and support various causes, including the Black Lives Matter movement.

Their influence extends to business ventures as well. Jay-Z's super-successful Roc Nation has become a powerhouse in the entertainment industry, representing some of the biggest names in music and sports. He also brought the Nets basketball team to Brooklyn.

Beyoncé, through her company Parkwood Entertainment, has produced critically acclaimed projects like *Homecoming*, a documentary about her historic Coachella performance. She and Jay-Z became the first billionaire couple in 2017 with an estimated net worth of US$1.6 bn.

Beyoncé and Jay-Z attend 2020 Roc Nation *The Brunch* on 25 January, 2020 in Los Angeles

As a couple, they've also ventured into philanthropy. Through initiatives like the Shawn Carter Foundation and the BeyGOOD Foundation, they have provided scholarships, disaster relief, and support for underserved communities. Their commitment to giving back is a reflection of their belief in using their success to uplift others. In this vein they also galvanised politics encouraging people to come out and vote for US President Barack Obama in 2008. Beyoncé went on to perform at both his inauguration ceremonies in 2009 and 2013.

Jay-Z collects an award at The 1998 Billboard Music Awards

Inside track on rapper and music mogul Jay-Z

Shawn Corey Carter, better known by his stage name Jay-Z, is one of the most influential and successful figures in the history of hip-hop – named the greatest rapper of all time in 2023 by Billboard.

Born on 4 December 1969, in Brooklyn, New York, Jay-Z rose from the streets of the Marcy Projects of Brooklyn, an environment fraught with crime and poverty, to become a global icon, not just in music but also in business, fashion, and philanthropy. His journey from hustler to billionaire entrepreneur and cultural leader is an illustration of his relentless drive, talent, and vision.

His early life experiences shaped much of his music, which often reflects the struggles and aspirations of urban life. He began rapping in the late 1980s and, after failing to secure a record deal, co-founded his own label, Roc-A-Fella Records, in 1995, with Damon Dash and Kareem 'Biggs' Burke. This move was the beginning of Jay-Z's entrepreneurial approach to his career, a trait that would define much of his success.

In 1996, Jay-Z released his debut album, *Reasonable Doubt*. Though it was not an immediate commercial success, it is now considered one of the greatest hip-hop albums of all time. Songs like *Dead Presidents II* and *Can't Knock the Hustle* introduced his unique blend of street narratives and aspirational themes with lyrical prowess and sophisticated storytelling.

His breakthrough came in 1998 with his third album, *Vol. 2... Hard Knock Life*, which included the smash hit *Hard Knock Life (Ghetto Anthem)*. This album propelled him to mainstream success, earning him his first Grammy Award and recognition as one of hip-hop's leading figures.

Jay-Z rose from the streets of the Marcy Projects of Brooklyn

Over the next decade, Jay-Z released a string of successful albums, including *The Blueprint* (2001) and *The Black Album* (2003), both of which are considered classics in the genre. *The Blueprint* was particularly significant for its soulful production and the fact that it was released on 11 September 2001, (9/11) a date that added an unintended layer of poignancy to its themes of resilience and survival.

Albums like *The Blueprint 3* (2009) and *Magna Carta Holy Grail* (2013) ensured his continuing relevance in an ever-changing industry, blending contemporary sounds with his established lyrical style. His 2017 album *4:44* is a deeply personal reflection on his life, exploring themes of legacy, family, and redemption.

These days his influence extends far beyond music. He is a savvy businessman who has built a vast empire, including ventures in fashion, sports, technology, and spirits. In 1999, he co-founded Rocawear, a hugely successful clothing line that earned him millions. He sold the rights to the brand for $204 million in 2007.

In 2003, Jay-Z ventured into the sports industry by purchasing a stake in the New Jersey Nets, later helping to relocate the team to Brooklyn as the Brooklyn Nets. He also founded Roc Nation in 2008, a full-service entertainment company that manages artists, athletes, and other talent. Roc Nation has become one of the most influential companies in the entertainment industry, managing superstars like Rihanna and J. Cole.

Jay-Z's business acumen is perhaps best exemplified by his investments in technology and spirits. In 2015, he acquired the streaming service Tidal, positioning it as a platform owned by artists for artists. He also invested in the Armand de Brignac champagne brand, known as Ace of Spades, which became synonymous with luxury and success in hip-hop culture.

Jay Z, Beyoncé and Win Butler of Arcade Fire attend the Tidal launch event on 30 March, 2015 in New York City

By 2019 these booming business ventures saw Jay-Z become a billionaire – one of only a handful of musicians and the first hip hop artist ever to achieve such status – a milestone that reflects his success not just in music, but across multiple industries.

Jay-Z's impact on culture is profound. He has been a voice for the African American community, addressing issues of race and inequality in his music and public statements.

Beyond music and business, Jay-Z has also made significant contributions to philanthropy, particularly through the Shawn Carter Foundation, which provides scholarships and support to underprivileged youth.

Beyoncé:

Introducing Sasha Fierce

Chapter 5

Beyoncé's 'Sasha Fierce' persona is one of the most intriguing and iconic elements of her career – a bold and daring alter ego that allowed her to explore new facets of her artistry.

One of the most significant reinventions of any artist ever, Sasha Fierce was introduced to the world through Beyoncé's third studio album, *I Am... Sasha Fierce*, released on 18 November 2008, just months after her wedding.

By introducing Sasha Fierce, Beyoncé wasn't just unveiling a new stage persona – she was launching a whole new era of her career. Sasha Fierce was bold, unapologetic, and fiercely confident, embodying a side of Beyoncé that was more daring and adventurous than the reserved and polished image she had previously presented. Beyoncé described Sasha as the 'fun, more sensual, more aggressive, more outspoken' version of herself. This duality allowed her to explore different facets of her identity and artistry and was also a response to the pressures of fame, allowing her to separate her personal life from her public persona.

I Am... Sasha Fierce was similarly in two parts, designed to highlight the dichotomy between Beyoncé's private and public personas. The first, *I Am...*, focused on Beyoncé's vulnerable and introspective side, featuring ballads and mid-tempo tracks that delved into themes of love, heartbreak, and self-reflection. The second disc, *Sasha Fierce*, was where her alter ego came to life, offering up-tempo, club-ready tracks.

The album was a commercial and critical success, debuting at #1 on the Billboard 200 chart, reaching #2 in the UK and earning numerous accolades, including six Grammy Awards.

Sasha Fierce was bold, unapologeitc, and Fiercely confi

Beyoncé Hits a Perfect Six and sweeps the Grammys

Beyoncé was among the top winners of the night at the 52nd Annual Grammy Awards in 2010, picking up a record for the most wins by a female artist in one night and bringing her career total to 16. Her prizes came for:

Song of the Year for *Single Ladies (Put a Ring on It)*

Best Female Pop Vocal Performance for *Halo*

Best Female R&B Vocal Performance for *Single Ladies (Put a Ring on It)*

Best Traditional R&B Vocal Performance for *At Last*

Best R&B Song for *Single Ladies (Put a Ring on It)*

Best Contemporary R&B Album for *I Am... Sasha Fierce*

Beyoncé accepts one of her 6 awards of the night at the 2010 Grammys

The album's impact extended beyond music, influencing fashion, pop culture, and the broader conversation around female empowerment.

In terms of style, Sasha Fierce was all about making a statement. Think edgy, glamorous, and slightly futuristic. Leather bodysuits, thigh-high boots, and bold accessories became her trademarks, creating a look that screamed power and confidence. The fashion choices were sharp and structured, with an emphasis on strong silhouettes that highlighted her figure and made her presence impossible to ignore.

One of the most striking elements of Sasha Fierce's look was the glove – specifically, the single, often metallic or jewel-encrusted, glove she wore on her left hand. More than a mere fashion statement, the glove was a symbol of the character's uniqueness and strength, adding an extra layer of mystique and authority to her performances, almost like a superhero's signature accessory. It differentiated Sasha Fierce from Beyoncé herself, visually signalling that when the glove was on, Sasha was in control.

Performance-wise, Sasha Fierce brought a palpable intensity to the stage. Beyoncé, as Sasha, delivered more aggressive dance moves, and her stage presence was electrifying. The choreography was sharper, and the energy was turned up several notches, making every performance feel like a fierce, high-octane experience as Beyoncé expressed her wilder side, pushing the boundaries of her artistry while still staying true to the core of who she is as a performer. Incorporating Sasha, Beyoncé's 2009-2010 'I Am... World Tour' was a total triumph.

Beyoncé decided to retire Sasha Fierce after that tour because she felt that she no longer needed to separate her on-stage persona from her true self. As Beyoncé grew more comfortable in her own skin and more confident in her abilities, she realised that she didn't need an alter ego to express those qualities. She had fully integrated the power and confidence of Sasha Fierce into her everyday persona. Beyoncé explained in interviews that she had reached a point in her life where she felt strong and confident in her own right, without needing to step into 'Sasha' to navigate the complexities of fame, identity, and self-expression.

In many ways, Sasha Fierce was a transitional figure in Beyoncé's career. She allowed Beyoncé to explore new creative territories and push the boundaries of her artistry. This exploration paved the way for future projects like *Beyoncé* (2013) and *Lemonade* (2016), where Beyoncé fully embraced her multifaceted identity, blending vulnerability with power, and personal narrative with social commentary.

Beyoncé performs onstage during the *I AM... World Tour* at Madison Square Garden on 22 June, 2009

I Am ...Sasha Fierce ▲

Released November 2008

I Am...

Characterised by its introspective and personal tone, the music on the 'I Am...' disc reflects Beyoncé's more vulnerable and emotional side, offering a glimpse into her thoughts on love, relationships, and self-discovery. The production on this portion of the album is generally more subdued, allowing Beyoncé's voice and the emotional weight of the lyrics to take centre stage.

Track listing

If I Were a Boy
Halo
Disappear
Broken-Hearted Girl
Ave Maria
Smash Into You
Satellites
That's Why You're Beautiful

Sasha Fierce...

The 'Sasha Fierce' side is where Beyoncé's alter ego truly comes to life. The music here is bold, energetic, and unapologetic, reflecting the confidence and assertiveness that Sasha Fierce embodies.

Track listing

Single Ladies (Put a Ring on It)
Radio
Diva
Sweet Dreams
Video Phone
Hello
Ego
Scared of Lonely

The Sasha Fierce era of work helped solidify Beyoncé's status as a global superstar, capable of influencing not just the music industry but also fashion, culture, and social discourse. The album's blend of introspection and boldness, vulnerability and confidence, set a new standard pop stardom in the 21st century.

It also demonstrated that an alter ego could be more than just a gimmick; it could be a powerful tool for artistic expression and exploration.

Beyoncé performing *Single Ladies* during the 2008 American Music Awards

Beyoncé:

The Evolution of an Artis[t] — 4 and Beyond

Chapter 6

Beyoncé's career has been marked by constant evolution, and her fourth studio album, *4,* released on 24 June 2011, was a significant milestone in this journey. With this album, Beyoncé stepped into a new era of creative control and artistic maturity, and began a more mature, experimental, and introspective phase of her career.

Marking a departure from the high-energy pop anthems that had characterised much of Beyoncé's earlier work, *4* leaned heavily into R&B, soul, and funk influences.

Tracks like *Love On Top*, with its infectious key changes, and *1+1*, a raw and passionate ballad, highlighted her ability to fuse traditional and contemporary sounds.

4 ▸

Released on 24 June 2011

Track listing

1+1
I Care
I Miss You
Best Thing I Never Had
Party (Ft. André 3000)
Rather Die Young
Start Over
Love On Top
Countdown
End of Time
I Was Here
Run the World (Girls)

Although the album didn't produce as many chart-topping singles as her previous releases, it was a commercial success, debuting at #1 on the Billboard 200, and was praised by critics, particularly for vocals and production. *4* also solidified Beyoncé's reputation as an artist who wasn't afraid to take risks and prioritise artistic integrity over commercial appeal. This album was a clear indicator that Beyoncé was beginning to focus more on the quality and message of her music rather than just chasing hits.

In many ways, *4* was a personal declaration of independence as it was Beyoncé first major project without her father Mathew's management. She had taken a break in 2010 after years of non-stop work and used the time to reflect on her personal priorities. As well as achieving her goal of what she described as doing 'random things....restaurants, maybe take a class, see some movies and Broadway shows', she also reassessed her professional relationships her career and eventually decided that she wanted to take full responsibility for her career – which meant leaving her father's management.

Beyoncé's professional relationship with her father, who had managed her career from the start, had begun to show signs of strain since her marriage and the decision to part ways business-wise in 2011 was driven by a combination of factors, both personal and professional.

Mathew's hands on management style reportedly became limiting as Beyoncé wanted to explore different creative directions as she entered a new phase in her life, marked by her marriage and the prospect of starting a family.

In March 2011 Beyoncé released a statement saying she and her father had 'parted ways', though 'only' on a business level. 'He is my father for life and I love my dad dearly. I am grateful for everything he has taught me...I grew up watching him and my mother manage their own businesses. They were hardworking entrepreneurs and I will continue to follow in their footsteps.'

Mathew also issued a statement saying that the decision had been mutual. 'We did great things together and I know that she will continue to conquer new territories in music and entertainment.'

Despite these quite positive public announcements, there were further difficulties behind the scenes. Mathew and Tina had separated in 2010, around the time a paternity test showed that he had fathered a son, Nixon, with actress Alexsandra Wright and Beyoncé seemed to take her mother's side as the couple began divorce proceedings which were finalised in November 2011. There were also widely reported but unconfirmed rumours of a financial dispute between Beyoncé and her father.

In Beyoncé's 2013 documentary for HBO, *Life Is But A Dream, she* opened up about how severing her business relationship with Mathew had taken its toll on their personal relationship.

'I'm feeling very empty because of my relationship with my dad. And I'm so fragile at this point and I feel like my soul has been tarnished', she said.

'Life is unpredictable but I feel like I had to move on, and not work with my dad. And I don't care if I don't sell one record. It's bigger than the record, it's bigger than my career.

'I think one of the biggest reasons I decided it was time to manage myself was because at some point you need your support system. You need your family. When you're tryin' to have an everyday conversation with your parents you have to talk about scheduling, and you have to talk about your album, and performing and touring. It's just too stressful, and it really affects your relationship.

'I needed boundaries, and I think my dad needed boundaries. It's really easy to get confused with this world that's your job that you live and breathe every day all day, and you don't know when to turn it off. You need a break. I needed a break. I needed my dad.'

Beyoncé attends the HBO Documentary Film *Beyoncé: Life Is But A Dream* New York Premiere alongside HBO executives in 2013

However, since then Beyoncé and Mathew have since expressed love and respect for each other, indicating that their personal relationship has remained intact.

While the decision to part ways professionally was difficult, it was also a crucial step in Beyoncé's journey toward becoming the independent and powerful artist she is today. Not least because after parting ways with her father, Beyoncé established her own management and entertainment company Parkwood Entertainment, through which she fully controls her brand and career.

So the production of *4* was a deeply personal process for her. She served as an executive producer on the album, overseeing every aspect of its creation – from the writing and recording to the visual presentation. She collaborated closely with a select group of producers, ensuring that the album's sound aligned with her vision. This level of involvement was a clear departure from the more collaborative, producer-driven approach of her earlier albums. It was also a strong statement that Beyoncé was no longer just a performer but a full-fledged artist in control of her narrative.

The album's sound was more sophisticated and diverse, drawing from a wide range of influences, including Fela Kuti, The Jackson 5, and Prince. Beyoncé herself described *4* as a 'labour of love,' where she allowed herself to experiment with different musical styles and take creative risks that she might have avoided earlier in her career.

The album also reflected Beyoncé's growing confidence as an artist who could set trends rather than follow them.

One of the most significant aspects of *4* was its exploration of themes that would become central to Beyoncé's work in the years to come: motherhood, feminism, and self-reflection. At the time of the album's release, Beyoncé was newly married to Jay-Z and would soon announce her pregnancy with their first child, Blue Ivy. This life stage deeply influenced the album, particularly on tracks like *Countdown*, where she joyfully celebrated her love for her husband and the anticipation of becoming a mother.

Beyoncé headlines the Pyramid Stage at the Glastonbury Festival on 26 June, 2011, just days after her 4 album was released

She also explored her evolving views on feminism. While earlier in her career she had touched on these themes, *4* marked the beginning of a more explicit and nuanced engagement with feminist ideas. This was especially evident in *Run the World (Girls)*, where Beyoncé boldly declared that women are the ones who drive the world forward and set the stage for the more overtly feminist themes that would come to define her later work, particularly in albums like *Beyoncé* and *Lemonade*.

Self-reflection was another key theme on *4*. Tracks like *I Miss You* and *Best Thing I Never Had* delve into introspection and emotional complexity, reflecting Beyoncé's willingness to be vulnerable and honest in her music.

By the beginning of 2012, with *4* launched, and her new management plans in order, there was time for Beyoncé to step away from the business for a while to focus on the birth of her daughter Blue Ivy. In a statement announcing the arrival of their daughter, Beyoncé and Jay-Z said, 'Her birth was emotional and extremely peaceful, we are in heaven .... It was the best experience of our lives.'

But of course music was never far from her mind and her next release shook up the industry completely...

Beyoncé lovingly looks on as Jay-Z carries baby Blue Ivy Carter leaving the Meurice hotel in Paris, 4 June, 2012

Beyoncé:

The Visual Album Era – Beyoncé and Lemonade

Chapter 7

Beyoncé has always been ahead of the curve, but with the release of her self-titled album *Beyoncé* in 2013 and then *Lemonade* in 2016, she didn't just set trends – she redefined the entire music industry. These two albums marked the beginning of the 'Visual Album Era,' where Beyoncé blended music, film, and social commentary in a way that had never been seen before, so setting a new standard for what a music album could be.

In December 2013, Beyoncé pulled off one of the most audacious moves in music history. Without any prior announcement, she dropped her fifth studio album, *"Beyoncé,"* directly onto iTunes at midnight on Friday 13th. No marketing, no singles, no leaks – just 14 tracks and 17 accompanying music videos, all at once. The shockwaves were immediate. The industry had never seen anything like it, and Beyoncé's name dominated headlines across the globe. Within hours she was #1 on iTunes in 100 countries. Within three days, the album had sold over 800,000 copies worldwide, debuting at #1 on the Billboard 200 chart. This made her the first woman to reach the top of the charts with all five of her first studio albums.

More than just a clever marketing stunt, this surprise release was a statement of power and control. She wanted her album to be considered as an entire body of work and not judged by singles released piecemeal or, even worse, leaked.

In a later video about the making of the album she explained that she'd been keen to get fans to listen to a whole album, rather than getting caught up in the singles and the hype, saying, 'Theres so much that gets between the music and the artist and the fans...I just want this to come out when it's ready – and from me, to my fans...I feel like that's something that's lost in pop music'.

By bypassing the traditional promotional cycle, Beyoncé had also proved that she could rely solely on her name and her work to generate buzz and sales. The success of this release was unprecedented, and changed the game for other artists, who began to consider alternative, more creative methods for releasing and marketing their music too.

Beyoncé

Released December 2013

Track listing

Pretty Hurts

Haunted

Drunk in Love (Ft. Jay-Z)

Blow

No Angel

Partition

Jealous

Rocket

Mine (Ft. Drake)

XO

Flawless (Ft. Chimamanda Ngozi Adichie)

Superpower (Ft. Frank Ocean)

Heaven

Blue (Ft. Blue Ivy)

Deluxe tracks

Flawless' (Ft. Nicki Minaj)

Ring Off

Blow (Ft. Pharrell)

Standing On The Sun (Ft. Mr. Vegas)

Beyoncé meets fans outside of the release party for her *Beyoncé* album

But the revolutionary impact of *Beyoncé* wasn't just in its release strategy. The album itself was a groundbreaking piece of work. Each song was paired with a visually stunning video, creating a cohesive narrative that explored themes of feminism, love, sexuality, and self-empowerment. Tracks like *Pretty Hurts* critique society's obsession with physical perfection, while the song *Flawless* with its now-iconic line 'I woke up like this' became an anthem of self-love. Beyoncé used her platform to challenge traditional notions of beauty and to celebrate the diversity of women's bodies and experiences. *Drunk in Love* was the album's only major hit single, peaking at #2 on the *Billboard* Hot 100, but the album as a whole was critically praised as her 'magnum opus' with her 'bold' approach and musical scope, and vocals gaining special mention.

The album's visual format allowed Beyoncé to tell a deeper, more layered story, giving fans an immersive experience that extended beyond just the music. It heralded her transition to owning her 'world', talking directly to fans via her music and social media platforms as she eschewed the old traditional concepts of interaction.

As the dust settled, Beyoncé hit the road again, first with her 11-month long Mrs. Carter World Tour and then with Jay-Z in June 2014 for their joint, 20-date On the Run Tour.

Beyoncé was back to full fitness after her pregnancy. As the UK's Observer newspaper review put it when reviewing 'Mrs Carter', 'What makes this show's largely enervating juggernaut breathe is Beyoncé's tireless physical effort'. She must indeed have been tired though as on top of a gruelling tour she was juggling the demands of motherhood, having taken Blue Ivy on tour with her of course.

While all was going well professionally, there was some trouble personally. The incident between Beyoncé's sister Solange and husband Jay-Z in the lift after the May 2014 Met Gala gave rise to all sorts of gossip about what could possibly have been behind the fracas. Theories ranged from the professional (for example that she had

The album itself was a groundbreaking piece of work

Beyoncé attends a release party and screening for her new self-titled album *Beyoncé* at the School of Visual Arts Theater, 21 December, 2013 in New York City

left his Roc Nation label) to the personal in that she was defending Beyoncé after Jay-Z had been flirting with other women at the gala. There were so many question marks hanging over the 'lift incident,' not least how the footage came into the public domain in the first place.

Beyoncé navigated the whole ugly business with her usual serenity, then the silence broke with the statement acknowledging the speculation around what was described as an 'unfortunate incident'... continuing 'The most important thing is that the family has worked through it. Jay and Solange each assume their share of responsibility for what has occurred. They both acknowledge their role in this private matter that has played out in public. They have apologised to each other and we have moved forward as a united family...we have put this behind us and hope everyone else will do the same'.

So it was back to music – and another extraordinary release, her second visual album and sixth studio solo recording *Lemonade*.

If *Beyoncé* was revolutionary, then *Lemonade* was seismic. Released in April 2016, *Lemonade* was not just a collection of songs; it was a powerful cultural and political statement that addressed issues of race, gender, ancestry and identity with extraordinary boldness. Again it was released without prior warning, and this time she took control a stage further by releasing it on Jay-Z's Tidal platform.

Lemonade is often described as a concept album, telling the story of a woman's journey through betrayal, anger, forgiveness, and redemption. Certainly, in her most personal work to date, she delves into her marriage, addressing the emotional fallout from the rumoured infidelities of her husband Jay-Z, with some fury and explicit references (as in 'Becky with the good hair').

However, the album's narrative is not just about Beyoncé's story – it's a politically charged piece of work about the struggles and triumphs of Black women more broadly.

But it's also even more than that. As well as addressing the Black Lives Matter movement, by raging at racial injustices in the United States, Beyoncé celebrated Black womanhood, explored her own Southern roots, and provided a commentary on the experiences of Black women in America. From the poetic interludes to the imagery of African American history and culture, *Lemonade* is steeped in symbolism and meaning.

Critically, Lemonade was considered a masterpiece – praised for its boldness, artistic vision, and unflinching exploration of difficult topics.

Before the incident - all smiles for Jaz-Z and Beyoncé as they arrive at the 2014 Met Gala

By weaving her own experiences into these broader themes, Beyoncé created a piece of work that was not only artistically rich, but also socially relevant. She used her music to spark widespread discussion and debate, making the album a cultural touchstone that went beyond music.

However, even judged by its music alone, Lemonade was an amazing body of work, an impressive feat of intricate songwriting, referencing other musicians and writers, and varied styles from New Orleans jazz to blues, funk and country. Each of the album's 12 songs including the hits *Formation, Sorry, Hold Up, Freedom,* and *All Night*, had its own accompanying short film, plus the album's release was accompanied by a one-hour film that premiered on HBO, further enhancing its impact. Through stunning visuals, Beyoncé took viewers on a journey through various stages of emotional turmoil, before arriving at a place of healing. The film's use of symbolism, such as the recurring imagery of water, added layers of depth to the album's narrative.

Lemonade was nominated for nine Grammy Awards, including Album of the Year, Record of the Year, and Song of the Year, although rather controversially the album only won two on the night, Best Urban Contemporary Album and Best Music Video for *Formation*.

Formation named best music video ever

As well as winning a Grammy, Beyoncé's music video for *Formation* was named the best music video of all time by Rolling Stone magazine in 2021.

'If Beyoncé's self-titled visual album established her as one of the greatest artists of all time, her surprise-released *Formation* video (and ensuing album *Lemonade*) marked her as one of the most important,' said the accompanying editorial.

Beyoncé poses in the press room with her awards for Best Music Video for *Formation* and Best Urban Contemporary Album for *Lemonade* at The Grammy Awards in 2017

Lemonade ▸

Released April 2016

Track listing

Pray You Catch Me
Hold Up
Don't Hurt Yourself (Ft. Jack White)
Sorry
6 Inch (Ft. The Weeknd)
Daddy Lessons
Love Drought
Sandcastles
Forward (Ft. James Blake)
Freedom (Ft. Kendrick Lamar)
All Night
Formation (Album version)
Sorry (Original demo version)

it's clear that Beyonce transformed the music industry

One of the most compelling aspects of both *Beyoncé* and *Lemonade* is how Beyoncé seamlessly blends her personal narrative with broader social commentary. These albums are deeply personal, yet they speak to universal themes that resonate with a wide audience.

Beyoncé accepts the award for Best Urban Contemporary Album for *Lemonade* onstage during The Grammy Awards in 2017

The success of *Beyoncé* and *Lemonade* has had a lasting impact on the music industry, particularly in how albums are conceptualised and released. While Beyoncé didn't invent the visual album, but she certainly popularised it, setting a new standard for what a music release could entail.

The idea that an album could be a full sensory experience, rather than just a collection of songs, inspired a new wave of creativity in the industry. Artists like Janelle Monáe, Kanye West, and Frank Ocean have all released projects that blur the lines between music and film, a trend that can be traced back to Beyoncé's pioneering work.

Few music artists have had the kind of impact that Beyoncé enjoyed with *Beyoncé* and *Lemonade.* These albums weren't just commercial successes; they were cultural landmarks that redefined what it meant to be an artist in the 21st century.

Looking back on this era of her career, it's clear that Beyoncé transformed the music industry. She used her platform to tell stories that mattered, to inspire change, and to create art that would stand the test of time. In doing so, she became more than a pop star, but an acclaimed visionary artist.

Visual Albums: Merging Music with Cinematic Storytelling

A visual album takes the idea of a concept album up a notch by pairing every track with a feature-length film or music video. These visuals bring the album's theme to life, adding an extra layer to the listening experience. Think of it as a long-form music video that weaves multiple songs into one cohesive cinematic piece. While traditional concept albums are all about the audio, visual albums mix in the visual elements to elevate the entire artistic package.

Beyoncé:

Chapter 8

Activism and Social Justice - Using Her Platform for Change

With each project, performance, and public statement, Beyoncé reaffirms her dedication to making the world a better place.

Whether it's through her music, public statements, or actions, she consistently advocates for equality and justice. Her activism covers a wide range of causes, including racial equality, gender equality, and LGBTQ+ rights. Beyoncé's ability to blend her artistry with activism allows her to reach a broad audience and shine a spotlight on critical issues, particularly those affecting the Black community.

Her role in the Black Lives Matter movement has been profound. She has used her music, social media presence, and public appearances to support the movement. One of her most notable contributions was during the 2016 BET Awards, where she delivered a powerful performance of *Freedom* with Kendrick Lamar, highlighting the struggles and resilience of the Black community. She has also been vocal in gaining attention for victims of police brutality and systemic racism, consistently urging her followers to take action and stay informed.

In addition, Beyoncé and her husband, Jay-Z, have contributed financially to the movement, including substantial donations to bail funds for protesters and support for legal assistance initiatives. This financial backing has been crucial in sustaining the momentum of the movement and supporting those on the front lines of activism.

The release of *Formation* in 2016 marked a significant moment in Beyoncé's career and in the landscape of music and activism. The song and its accompanying video are rich with imagery and messages celebrating Black culture and addressing issues such as police brutality and racial inequality. Beyoncé's performance of Formation during the 2016 Super Bowl half-time show was a bold political statement, evoking the spirit of the civil rights movement of the 1950s and 60s.

Beyoncé and Kendrick Lamar perform onstage during the 2016 BET Awards

Formation single artwork

Smashing the Super Bowl

Beyoncé's performance at the Super Bowl XLVII halftime show in February 2013 is among the top 10 most watched of all time with 110 million viewers. She sang a medley of songs, some solo and some from Destiny's Child days as the band reunited on stage as a fan surprise.

Then in 2016, along with Bruno Mars she joined headliners Coldplay as guest artist for a surprise and, as it turned out, politically charged and controversial performance of her *Formation* track, in what was the most-watched programme of the year on American television.

Beyoncé, Chris Martin of Coldplay, and Bruno Mars, perform during halftime of Super Bowl 50 in 2016

Beyoncé's commitment to social justice extends beyond her music and performances. She is actively involved in philanthropy, supporting numerous causes through her BeyGOOD initiative. This foundation has provided financial aid to families affected by natural disasters, scholarships for students, and support for small businesses.

During the COVID-19 pandemic, BeyGOOD partnered with organisations to provide testing, healthcare, and financial assistance to vulnerable communities. Beyoncé has also supported campaigns for mental health awareness and gender equality.

In 2020, after the murder of African American George Floyd, Beyoncé spoke directly to her fans through social media and encouraged them to take action, sign petitions, and educate themselves on the relevant issues. Her consistent advocacy has made her a trusted and influential figure.

Beyoncé's influence now extends far beyond the United States. Respected as a music artist, businesswoman, actress and mother, her activism has received international recognition and inspired movements around the globe. She has been named one of Time magazine's 100 most influential people multiple times, highlighting her impact not just as an artist but as a global advocate for change. As the cover star of the 2014 issue she was profiled by Sheryl Sandberg, then COO of Facebook who wrote, 'Beyoncé doesn't just sit at the table. She builds a better one.'

Her work has also been recognized by various humanitarian and civil rights organizations. For example, in 2019, she received the Image Award for Entertainer of the Year, from the NAACP (National Association for the Advancement of Colored People) the oldest American civil rights organisation, and dedicated her award to the beauty of being Black, while also taking time to celebrate the accomplishments of other Black artists and activists.

'Beyoncé doesn't just sit at the table. She builds a better one.'

Beyoncé:

Business Mogul - Buildin[g] a Brand Beyond Music

Chapter 9

s well as commanding the stage, Beyoncé is just as powerful behind the scenes, building an empire that extends far beyond music.

Her journey as a business mogul began alongside her musical career. Known for her meticulous attention to detail and strategic thinking, she has seamlessly transitioned from global superstar to formidable entrepreneur. Her business acumen is evident in every project she undertakes, from her music releases to her ventures in fashion, film, and beyond.

As she told *GQ* magazine in a 2024 interview, 'There's a huge contrast between the business journeys of men and women. Men often have the luxury of being perceived as the strategists, the brains behind their ventures. They're given the space to focus on the product, the team, the business plan. Women, on the other hand, especially those in the limelight, are frequently pigeonholed into being the face of the brand or the marketing tool. It's important to me to continue to take the same approach I have taken with my music and apply my learnings to my businesses.'

One of the keys to Beyoncé's success is her hands-on approach. She is deeply involved in the creative and business aspects of her projects, ensuring that her brand remains authentic and true to her vision. This dedication has not only solidified her reputation as an artist but also as a businesswoman who understands the importance of controlling her narrative and brand image. Preferring to speak directly to fans, she does very few traditional media interviews. As she explained in the 2024 piece for *GQ* magazine, she's keen to ensure that her personal life doesn't turn into a brand.

'One thing I've worked extremely hard on is making sure my kids can have as much normalcy and privacy as possible,' she said. 'It's very easy for celebrities to turn our lives into performance art. I have made an extreme effort to stay true to my boundaries and protect myself and my family. No amount of money is worth my peace.'

Her business acumen is evident in every project she undertakes

She went on to say that the only part of her life that 'can at times feel like prison' is the fame that comes with the business, which is why she stays under the radar when she has nothing to promote. 'So, when you don't see me on red carpets, and when I disappear until I have art to share, that's why,' she added.

One of her most notable business ventures is Ivy Park, her athleisure brand. Launched in 2016 in partnership with Topshop, Ivy Park combines fashion and fitness, offering stylish and functional athletic wear. Beyoncé took full ownership of the brand in 2018, severing ties with Topshop's parent company Arcadia Group.

Beyoncé's Ivy Park collection goes on sale at Topshop on April 14, 2016 in London

In 2019, Ivy Park relaunched in collaboration with Adidas, marking a new era for the brand. The collections have been incredibly successful, often selling out within minutes of release.

Another cornerstone of her empire is Parkwood Entertainment, founded by Beyoncé in 2010. Originally a production and management company, Parkwood has evolved into a multifaceted entertainment powerhouse, handling everything from music production and film projects to talent management and creative direction. It's Beyoncé's main vehicle for maintaining creative control and pushing the boundaries of traditional entertainment.

Most recently she launched a whisky, SirDavis, created in partnership with Moët Hennessy, and named after her great-grandfather, Davis Hogue.

Beyoncé has made significant strides in film production as well. She has starred in and produced several films, including the live-action remake of *The Lion King*, where she voiced Nala and curated the companion album, *The Lion King: The Gift*.

As she continues to innovate and expand her empire, Beyoncé remains a powerful example of what it means to be a business mogul in the modern era.

Beyoncé celebrates the launch of her hair care line, Cécred, with an intimate gathering at he Revery LA, 20 February, 2024

Beyoncé and Kelly Rowland attend the SirDavis American Whisky Launch Party in Paris, 23 September, 2024

Beyoncé:

Coachella and Renaissance

Chapter 10

After *Lemonade* in 2016, Beyoncé kept fans waiting six years for new solo music. But in the meantime she was busy working on other landmark projects and performances.

One of the most important of these was her April 2018 headline performance at Coachella – one of the most famous festivals in the world – which was widely praised as 'historic'.

As the first black woman ever to headline the festival, Beyoncé gave a commanding performance, positioned as a celebration of Black culture, in particular the traditions of America's Historically Black Colleges and Universities (HBCUs).

Featuring a marching band, steppers, and a choir, all of which are staples of Black college life, Beyoncé's performance was rich with symbolism and references to Black history, including nods to Black leaders and movements.

The stage was transformed into a massive pyramid with a bleacher-style sports arena seating setup, reminiscent of a homecoming celebration at an HBCU. The choreography, led by a large ensemble of dancers, was intricate and dynamic, blending assorted styles from traditional African dance to modern hip-hop. Beyoncé's costumes, also paying homage to HBCUs, were custom-made by Balmain and included a yellow crop top and denim shorts, a sequined camo bodysuit, and a pink sweatshirt with fringe boots.

One of the night's most exciting moments came when former Destiny's Child bandmates Kelly Rowland and Michelle Williams joined Beyoncé on stage for a surprise reunion and the three reprised some of their biggest hits.

Now forever known as 'Beychella', the dazzling show is remembered as one of the most memorable live performances in music history, not only for its scale and execution but also for its powerful celebration of Black culture and its profound impact on the festival landscape.

The Coachella performance was streamed live on YouTube where is set a viewing record, with over 458,000 concurrent viewers, the highest ever for Coachella and one of the biggest live streams in YouTube history at the time. It was also recorded for a Netflix special and a live album, both called *Homecoming*.

Also in 2018, Beyoncé and Jay-Z, together credited as the 'Carters' released their first joint album, *Everything is Love* which they went on to perform during their On The Run II Tour. The hip hop and R&B tracks explored everything from love to fame, to Black pride. It debuted at #2 on the Billboard 200 and won the 2019 Grammy award for best urban contemporary album.

Michelle Williams, Beyoncé Knowles and Kelly Rowland of Destiny's Child perform onstage during the Coachella 2018

Then in June 2020, amid the protests and outrage surrounding the murder of George Floyd, an African American man killed by a white police officer in Minneapolis, Beyoncé surprise released a single, *Black Parade*, using her platform in support of Black activism, demanding justice and celebrating Black culture. The track went on to win Best R&B performance at the 2021 Grammy awards, making Beyoncé the most awarded female artist in Grammy history with 28 wins.

An extended version of *Black Parade* was used during the credits of Beyoncé's 2020 film *Black Is King*.

On a more up-beat note, Beyoncé received her first Oscar nomination in 2022. *Be Alive*, from the film 'King Richard', a biopic about the father of tennis superstars Venus and Serena Williams, was recognised in the Best Original Song category. She opened the show in a pre-recorded performance filmed on the tennis courts where Venus and Serena first played, wearing a tennis ball-inspired yellow neon gown, featuring sequins and feathers, designed by David Koma.

Then her fans got what they had truly been waiting for – her seventh solo studio album, *Renaissance* – her most ambitious musical project to date. This was a pure 'wall of sound' dance album, celebrating the contributions of Black and queer innovators, conceived during the 2020 Covid lockdowns which allowed Beyoncé an uninterrupted creative period.

Instead of dropping the album as a surprise as she had done before, Beyoncé spent six weeks promoting it more traditionally, including giving a rare interview to British *Vogue*.

The magazine's editor-in-chief Edward Enninful became one of the very first people to hear the new album, describing 'soaring vocals and fierce beats' that reminded him 'of the clubs of the 1980s and 90s'.

The most awarded female artist in Grammy history

Beyoncé wins the award for Best R&B Performance at The Grammy Awards, 14 March, 2021

The album paid tribute to house and disco music, and its queer history. Beyoncé dedicated the album to her late gay Uncle Johnny, whom she described as '... my godmother and the first person to expose me to a lot of the music and culture that serve as inspiration for this album.'

Another bold release, Renaissance covers numerous genres – disco, funk, techno, hip-hop, house, dancehall, Afrobeats and ballroom – as well as references to African American dance music creators and LGBTQI+ dancehall culture.

It also acknowledges the work of 1970s disco diva Donna Summer and bounce-music star Big Freedia.

An extensive list of collaborators including singers, writers and producers included Grace Jones, Drake, The-Dream, Pharrell Williams, Honey Dijon, Skrillex, BloodPop, Syd, Hit-Boy, Mike Dean and A.G. Cook.

Explaining more about the album on an Instagram post, Beyoncé said, 'Creating this album allowed me a place to dream and to find escape during a scary time for the world. It allowed me to feel free and adventurous in a time when little else was moving.

'My intention was to create a safe place, a place without judgment, a place to be free of perfectionism and overthinking. A place to scream, release, feel freedom. It was a beautiful journey of exploration. I hope you find joy in this music. I hope it inspires you to release the wiggle. Ha! And to feel as unique, strong, and sexy as you are.'

She also said that Renaissance was the first release from a 'three act project' she recorded during the pandemic and referred to the album as 'Act I.'

Explaining her decision to move away from the visual album format of *Lemonade*, Beyoncé told *GQ* magazine in 2024 that, 'I thought it was important that during a time where all we see is visuals, that the world can focus on the voice. The music is so rich in history and instrumentation. It takes months to digest, research, and understand.

'The music needed space to breathe. Sometimes a visual can be a distraction from the quality of the voice and the music," she added. "The years of hard work and detail put into an album that takes over four years! The music is enough. The fans from all over the world became the visual. We got the visual on tour and from my film'.

Renaissance was named album of the year on several 'best of' lists of 2022. It also made her the top nominee at the 2024 Grammys as her four wins (from nine nominations) on the night saw her become the top Grammy winner of all time with a total of 32 total awards.

Her wins that night were for Best Dance/Electronic Recording for *Break My Soul*, Best Dance/Electronic Album for *Renaissance*, Best Traditional R&B Performance for *Plastic Off the Sofa* and Best R&B Song with *Cuff It*.

Renaissance ▸

Seventh solo album and first in planned trilogy, 29 July 2022

Track listing

I'm That Girl
Cozy
Alien Superstar
Cuff It
Energy (Ft. Beam)
Break My Soul
Church Girl
Plastic Off the Sofa
Virgo's Groove
Move (Ft. Grace Jones & Tems)
Heated
Thique
All Up in Your Mind
America Has a Problem
Pure/Honey
Summer Renaissance

Beyoncé on the Renaissance World Tour at Tottenham Hotspur Stadium in London, 1 June, 2023

Beyoncé:

Touring the world

Chapter 11

Beyoncé's artistry is never more evident than when she performs live on stage and she goes bigger and gets better with every tour. From the earliest days of solo performing she has been committed to providing her 'Beyhive' of fans with a visually stunning and emotionally resonant experience.

Here's a rundown of her touring history, post Destiny's Child:

The Beyoncé Experience (2007) ▼

Beyoncé's first solo tour after Destiny's Child supported her second studio album, *B'Day*, which showed her growth as a solo artist, established her as a powerhouse solo performer and launched her all female live band Suga Mama.

The set list included tracks from her two solo albums, plus a Destiny's Child medley and the track *Listen* from Beyoncé's movie *Dreamgirls*.

The stage featured a sleek, minimalist design that put the focus firmly on Beyoncé who dazzled in multiple costumes featuring sequins, sparkles, and luxurious fabrics in red, black and silver. Critics loved her look with one exclaiming that she appeared as a 'glittering goddess' while another said the sight of her in a 'barely there' bodysuit '...will linger in my memory for years to come'. It nudged US$25m in gross earnings.

I Am... World Tour (2009-2010) ▼

Supporting the *I Am... Sasha Fierce* album, this tour was her biggest to date. A huge step up, it spanned five legs across six continents which saw her give over 100 performances and reach more than a million fans worldwide. It grossed around US$100m. She aimed to make it more emotional than The Beyoncé Experience in order to reflect the "real, raw and more sensitive" nature of the *I Am...* portion of the double album the tour was based around.

The slick show featured two stages, one centred around a massive staircase. The costumes by Thierry Mugler were a significant highlight, ranging from glamorous gowns to edgy, urban looks, reflecting the different themes of her performance.

The Mrs. Carter Show World Tour (2013-2014) ▶

Celebrating her married name, this tour supported her self-titled album *Beyoncé* and was one of her most successful ever, grossing over $229 million.

Featuring royal themes with Beyoncé emulating different queens through her costume choices, Beyoncé dazzled in a mix of high-fashion and theatrical costumes, including creations by Givenchy, Emilio Pucci, and David Koma. Memorable outfits included a crystal-embellished bodysuit, a gold sequined jumpsuit, and a Victorian-inspired gown with intricate lace detailing.

The 2013 shows included songs from all four of her solo studio albums, while the set list for later shows was revised to incorporate tracks from her eponymous fifth album. Her husband Jay-Z made multiple guest appearances.

On the Run Tour (2014) (with Jay-Z) ▼

This co-headlining stadium tour with her husband Jay-Z, focussed on North America, with some additional shows in Paris. The tour was a commercial success, grossing $96 million in the first 19 North American shows alone. The theme of being 'on the run' referenced their early 2000s '03 Bonnie and Clyde' collaboration. The couple performed together and separately; '... the coordination is not just remarkable, it's the absolute best way that two of the world's best performers can deliver a show that proves why they're on top together,' said the review from USA Today.

Beyoncé's most notable costumes included a black-and-white American flag outfit with a 16.4ft long train designed by Riccardo Tisci of Givenchy and a black bodysuit using fishnet and leather, by Versace.

Beyoncé's Suga Mama: The Powerhouse All-Female Band

'Suga Mama' is an all-female band that played a crucial role in Beyoncé's earlier live performances, bringing a celebration of female talent and artistry to the stage. Formed in 2006, the group varied between nine to 12 members at different times, all accomplished female musicians including percussionists, guitarists, saxophonists, and keyboard players. There was also a trio of background vocalists called The Mamas.

Named after her track *Suga Mama* on the *B'Day* album, the band's powerful performances blended seamlessly with Beyoncé's vocals, creating an electrifying and cohesive live experience. Their very presence onstage highlighted Beyoncé's dedication to supporting women in the music industry. 'I just wanted to do something which would inspire other young females to get involved in music,' Beyoncé said.

The group disbanded after the 2014 On The Run tour, although some of the members still feature in Beyoncé's touring bands, including on the 2023 Renaissance tour.

'Suga Mama,' the American all-female live performance band in 2009

The Formation World Tour (2016) ▼

Promoting the critically acclaimed *Lemonade*, this 40-plus-date world tour was one of the highest-grossing of 2016, earning over $256 million. Its production values were off the scale, the centrepiece of the stage being a giant rotating cubed video screen towering 60ft high, as well as a massive treadmill, and a pool of water for the finale.

Take fierce, fast pin-sharp and complex choreography as a given, with Beyoncé performing her usual astounding vocal acrobatics for an eclectic mix of numbers old and new.

Beyoncé's costumes for this tour were bold and politically charged. Highlights included a black and gold military-inspired bodysuit by Balmain, a red latex bodysuit by Atsuko Kudo, and custom pieces by Roberto Cavalli.

On the Run II Tour (2018) (with Jay-Z) ▼

Another joint tour with Jay-Z, supporting their debut collaborative album *Everything Is Love*. On the Run II Tour spanned Europe and North America and was a commercial success, grossing over $253 million.

For this joint tour with Jay-Z, Beyoncé's costumes were both glamorous and edgy. Designers like LaQuan Smith, Versace, and Alexander Wang contributed to her wardrobe. Standout looks included a metallic bodysuit, a leather trench coat with matching thigh-high boots, and a beaded, fringed mini dress.

Renaissance World Tour (2023) ▼

Supporting her seventh studio album *Renaissance*, this all-stadium tour marked Beyoncé's return to live performances after the pandemic and was one of the most ambitious of her entire career. Highlighting her evolution as an artist, she gave tour de force performances which included treating fans to her first visual interpretation of tracks like *Break My Soul, Alien Superstar* and *Cuff It*. Her 2.5 to 3 hours long set included 36 songs, a perfect mix of numbers from each of her other albums as well as the *Renaissance* tracks. There were some nine costume changes – each a bespoke creation from an impressive list of couture contributors including Balmain, Courrèges, Mugler and Valentino, accessorised by Tiffany & Co jewellery which even included a custom-made earpiece sparkling with diamonds.

Her highest-grossing tour to date (US$580million) and the highest grossing ever by a Black artist, it comprised 56 shows running from May to October 2023. The hugely impressive staging, featuring high spec and ultraviolet technology and a stand of hydraulic robotic arms, also included monumental sculptures, metallic tanks, mannequin-horses and pyrotechnics – all combining to make a breathtaking and grand visual spectacle.

Beyoncé:

Chapter 12

As well as entertaining millions with her music, Beyoncé has also taken lead and supporting roles in movies, gaining 10 acting-related award nominations in the process, adding to the hundreds she has received for her musical work.

Carmen Brown in *Carmen: A Hip Hopera* (2001)

Beyoncé's first-ever acting role saw her working alongside Wyclef Jean, Bow Wow, Jermaine Dupri and Mos Def as budding actress Carmen Brown in a reworking of the 19th century opera *Carmen*.

Foxxy Cleopatra - Austin Powers in *Goldmember* (2002)

Playing a law enforcement officer in this comedy franchise, Beyoncé teamed up with Mike Myers to thwart the plans of the evil supervillain Dr Evil.

Beyoncé Knowles & Sir Michael Caine during *Austin Powers in Goldmember* - New York Screening After-Party

Lily in *The Fighting Temptations* (2003)

As choir member and single mother Lilly, Beyoncé was the love interest of this film's star Cuba Gooding Jr. playing New York City advertising executive Darrin Hill who, after losing his job, returns to his hometown in Georgia, and takes over the local church choir.

Xania in *The Pink Panther* (2006)

Playing a popstar suspected of stealing the famous Pink Panther diamond, Beyoncé was a great foil for comedian Steve Martin as Inspector Clouseau in this reworking of the 1963 original.

Deena Jones – *Dreamgirls* (2006)

As Deena, the lead singer of a fictional girl group from Detroit – based on Diana Ross and the Supremes and their Motown record label – Beyoncé could draw on all her performance experiences for this adaptation of the 1981 Broadway musical.

Etta James – *Cadillac Records* (2008)

Beyoncé received NAACP and Satellite Image Award nominations for Best Supporting Actress for her performance as award-winning ballad and blues singer Etta James in this biopic about the founder of her label Chess Records.

Beyoncé during *Dreamgirls* Los Angeles Premiere in Beverly Hills, California

Sharon in *Obsessed* (2009)

Beyoncé plays the wife of financial company boss Derek Charles (Idris Elba), who is being pursued by a psychotic employee, intent on ending his marriage.

Queen Tara in *Epic* (2013)

Beyoncé voiced the 'Queen Tara, ruler of the Forest' character in this animated adaptation of the children's book *The Leaf Men and the Brave Good Bugs*.

Nala in *The Lion King* (2019)

Beyoncé voiced lioness Nala – Simba's childhood friend and future love interest – in this live action animated remake of the Disney classic. She was Grammy-nominated and Golden Globe-nominated for the song *Spirit* which she co-wrote for the movie. She also produced and curated the album *The Lion King: The Gift*, a collection of songs inspired by the film and including *Spirit*. *The Lion King* further inspired her 2020 film/visual album *Black is King* which she wrote and directed as an exploration of African heritage and identity themes.

She reprised her role as Nala in the new 2024 *Mufasa: The Lion King*.

Concert films and documentaries:

Beyoncé: I Am...World Tour (2010)

Capturing all the action from her 110-show world tour, Beyoncé directed this film including concert footage from multiple shows. It also featured sections showing elements of her private life which she personally filmed.

Beyoncé: Year of 4 (2011)

This 20-minute YouTube documentary, kicked off Beyoncé's documentary-making career as it chronicled the year of 2011 when she made her album *4*, showing personal and professional glimpses of her life at that time. She referenced the 'scary but empowering' decision to look after her own career, breaking away from her father's management.

Beyoncé: Life Is But a Dream (2013)

This film, a follow up to *Beyoncé: Year of 4,* was expanded to include the birth of Blue Ivy Carter in 2012. In some very personal revelations Beyoncé said that she had suffered a miscarriage around the time that *4* was released. The film also includes concert footage from her May 2012 4-night residency at Revel Atlantic City.

Beyoncé Presents: Making The Gift (2019)

As the title says, this 40-minute documentary is a straightforward, track by track examination of her 'love letter to Africa' album *The Lion King: The Gift*.

Beyoncé at *The Lion King* European Premiere in 2019

Homecoming: A Film by Beyoncé (2019)

Detailing her historic 2018 Coachella performances, Beyoncé showed seamlessly edited, in depth and intimate footage from across her shows. It's widely considered as among the all-time best concert films.

Black is King (2020)

Beyoncé co-wrote, executive produced, and directed this musical film conceived as a visual companion to her album *The Lion King: The Gift*

The film retells the story of the Disney classic, The Lion King, using the story of a young African prince reclaiming his thrown after first being exiled from his kingdom as an allegory for the African diaspora reclaiming and celebrating their culture and heritage.

With a diverse cast and crew and countless opportunities given to new talent, all the music, choreography, costumes, hairstyling, and sets were specifically designed to showcase Black talent and African culture. The costume designs won an Emmy.

Renaissance: A Film by Beyoncé (2023)

Documenting the planning and execution of her album and world tour of the same name, *Renaissance: A Film by Beyoncé* featured guest appearances from husband Jay-Z and their children, along with Diana Ross, Megan Thee Stallion and Kendrick Lamar. Beyoncé wrote, produced and directed the film which included all the songs from the album, with other famous tracks, and mixed behind the scenes footage with concert performances. It grossed US$21m in its opening weekend.

Taylor Swift attends the London premiere of *Renaissance: A Film By Beyoncé* on November 30, 2023 in London

s widely considered as among the all-time best concert films

Beyoncé:

Motherhood and Legacy

Chapter 13

She's a powerhouse performer, a boundary-breaking artist, and a business mogul. But behind the scenes, another equally significant role defines her – being a mother.

Since welcoming daughter, Blue Ivy Carter in 2012 and twins Rumi and Sir Carter in 2017, motherhood has profoundly shaped Beyoncé's life and work, influencing everything from her music to her business ventures.

She has often spoken about how becoming a mother changed her perspective, making her more empathetic and nurturing, with a deeper sense of purpose and a renewed focus on her priorities.

'I want to create content that inspires and encourages my children, as well as other children, to know that they can grow up in a world where they look in the mirror, love what they see, and can do anything they want,' she told British Vogue in December 2020. 'It's important to me that they see themselves in books, films, and on the runways.'

Jay Z, Blue Ivy Carter and Beyoncé attend the 66th NBA All-Star Game in 2017

In this vein, Beyoncé's music increasingly reflects themes of family, ancestry and legacy. Songs like *Blue* and *Brown Skin Girl* (which featured both Blue Ivy and Rumi in its video) celebrate her children's identities and the beauty of Black heritage. And of course her visual album *Lemonade* explored the complexities of family dynamics, forgiveness, and the strength of women.

Although well known for maintaining a fierce level of privacy around her family life, Beyoncé has recently given fans rare glimpses into her relationship with her children and some insight around her day to day family life.

'Most days I try to wake up at around 6am, squeezing in an hour or two of work before the little ones are up,' she told *GQ* magazine in 2024. 'Parenting while working, I move forward, embracing the beauty and the chaos of it all.'

She tries to tour when her children are on school holidays so they can come with her and experience 'different languages, architecture, and lifestyles' and shared that they often join her while she's recording and working in her dance studio.

'Raising three kids isn't easy,' she continued in her GQ interview. 'The older they get, the more they become their own individuals with unique needs, hobbies, and social lives. Parenting constantly teaches you about yourself. It takes a lot of prayer and patience. I love it. It's grounding and fulfilling.'

Beyoncé and Blue Ivy Carter on 4 November, 2014 in New York City

A passion for fashion

Chapter 14

Beyoncé is a fashion powerhouse with influence extending far beyond the stage – everything she wears has an impact.

Her personal style is luxurious, yet accessible – a blend of glamour, sophistication, and boldness. Her off-duty casual looks often feature high-waisted jeans, stylish blazers, statement accessories, and designer handbags.

When it comes to the red carpet, Beyoncé's appearances are nothing short of spectacular. She often chooses daring outfits with sheer fabrics, mini dress silhouettes and thigh-high slits for eye-catching looks that wow audiences.

For concert performances, things go up another level. Beyoncé's stage costumes are a crucial part of her performance identity. Designed to enhance her shows' visual spectacle and reflect the themes of her music, Beyoncé's stage costumes are legendary for their boldness, creativity, and attention to detail. As an example of her impact, she gets the credit for popularising the now ubiquitous leotard as a performance outfit after wearing one in her *Single Ladies* video.

Everything is meticulously crafted to ensure maximum impact and designed to enhance her dynamic performances. These outfits often incorporate elements of haute couture and street fashion, blending elegance with edginess.

Collaborating with top designers like Balmain, Givenchy, and Versace, Beyoncé's costumes reflect her themes of resilience and cultural pride. Among her most famous looks are the military-inspired jackets from her 'Formation' tour, the Egyptian-inspired ensembles from Coachella 2018, and the futuristic bodysuits of 'The Mrs. Carter Show'. Each costume is a visual statement that complements her music and elevates her performances to unforgettable spectacles.

Beyoncé's showstopping looks in the film *Black is King* saw her named the most influential woman in fashion in 2020 by British fashion platform Lyst.

Further proof of her potent power as an influencer came when the release of *Cowboy Carter* in 2024 saw sales of Western-style fashion rocket, including huge surges in demand for cowboy hats and boots, denim flares, and fringed jackets.

Levi Stauss & Co even saw its stock price rise following her mention of the brand in her song *Levii's Jeans*.

She collaborates with top designers known for their creativity, craftsmanship, and ability to push the boundaries of fashion to create her unforgettable looks. Among her chosen designers are...

Balmain ▶

Beyoncé has a longstanding partnership and friendship with Balmain's creative director Olivier Rousteing, with the designer creating many of her stage costumes. His bold, structured designs and attention to detail make him a perfect match for Beyoncé's powerful performance style. She wore multiple Balmain pieces on the Renaissance tour including a custom caged pearl bodysuit, a mirrored and embellished mini dress, and a crystal and pearl embellished bodysuit.

Peter Dundas

With a glamorous, bohemian style which complements Beyoncé's versatility and elegance, Dundas has designed several memorable outfits for Beyoncé, including the stunning gold beaded 2017 Grammys gown she wore for her performance which was perfectly set off with a matching sun-inspired headpiece and gold cuff necklace. She later changed into another Dundas design, a red sequinned gown with a plunging neckline, which complementing her growing baby bump and showed off her 'glow' while she was pregnant with her twins.

Givenchy ▶

From a black and gold Givenchy gown with matching gold boots for the 2013 Met Gala, to a black tulle base mini dress with structured capped sleeves, sparkling with beads, stones, bugle beads and threaded chain loops, Givenchy's custom haute couture always works for Beyoncé. Riccardo Tisci, formerly of Givenchy, has designed numerous red carpet and stage looks for her with his ability to blend sensuality with sophistication aligning perfectly with her aesthetic. Beyoncé turned heads in a sheer, jewel-encrusted Givenchy gown by Tisci at the 2015 Met Gala, 'China: Through the Looking Glass'. The daring, body-hugging dress featured intricate beading and a dramatic train, making it one of the most talked-about looks of the night.

David Koma

The Georgian-born, London-based designer David Koma who was the creative director of fashion house Mugler from 2013 to 2017 and has his own namesake line, has long been a go-to for Beyoncé. The singer first wore a Koma dress in 2009, for the MTV Europe Music Awards.

He was involved with her Renaissance tour for which he designed several costumes, including the headline-making iridescent bodysuit with a detachable skirt-sarong with a matching long biker jacket and knee-high boots.

He also designed her outfit for the cover of the single *Texas Hold 'Em*.

Loewe

Loewe made a strong showing during the Renaissance tour where costumes included a custom-made, honey-coloured Loewe catsuit covered in an abstract handprint and a sparkly silver long sleeves and trousers suit, with a metal breastplate.

Elie Saab

Beyoncé has chosen designs by Lebanese designer Elie Saab for many red carpet appearances, including a glamorous gold gown for the 2007 Golden Globes, an ice blue-and-silver tulle and sequined strapless floor-length dress for the 2008 Grammys, and a curve-hugging beaded creation for the 2009 Golden Globes.

Versace ▶

Beyoncé often turns to Versace for both red carpet and stage looks. The brand's opulent, high-glamour designs are a natural fit for her larger-than-life persona. At the Vanity Fair Oscar Party in 2005, Beyoncé stunned in a strapless gown by Versace which highlighted her hourglass figure and added a touch of old Hollywood glamour to the event.

Valentino

The Valentino gown Beyoncé wore on her *Renaissance* tour involved 20 metres of ivory silk cady, 390,000 crystal rhinestones (1,000 of them hand-applied) and took a total of 30 hours to make, perfectly encapsulating the craft and painstaking detail that goes into an haute couture creation. It was accessorised with silver opera gloves, custom mirrored shoes and Tiffany & Co jewellery.

Emilio Pucci

Known for vibrant prints and luxurious fabrics, Emilio Pucci has created several standout looks for Beyoncé's tours. Their designs add a touch of playfulness and sophistication to her wardrobe.

Alexander McQueen

Beyoncé has worn McQueen on important occasions for years, including the Hollywood premiere of *The Lion King* in 2019 and for her cover of British Vogue in 2020. No surprise then that she chose the fashion house to make the costume for her opening number on the Renaissance tour – a body suit with matching ankle boots, sparkling with silver bugle bead and crystal anatomical embroidery, hand-stitched onto a black tulle base.

Mugler

In another knockout ensemble during the Renaissance tour, Beyoncé paid tribute to her 'Beyhive' of fans by wearing 'The Mugler Bee' corset inspired by a 1997 Mugler couture collection, Les Insectes.

Bey in boots ▶

Stylist Marni Senofonte, who worked with Beyoncé on her *Lemonade* HBO special and her *Formation* world tour, shared some backstage information on how Queen Bey manages to dance and quick change her trademark over the knee boots. Speaking to US publication Footwear News, Marni said that Beyoncé always has a thick heel of around 2.5-3ins to give the ankle support necessary for dancing. 'The problem with the boots is that we have to make a zipper, a full, complete zipper for fast changes – the boots have to come off easily. For over-the-knee styles, we add boning so they stay up.'

Beyoncé:
SiriusXM

Cowboy Carter and beyond

Chapter 15

Genre-defying as ever, Beyoncé ensured her eighth studio album came as a surprise to all as she entered the hallowed turf of 'country' music.

Hailed as a 'masterpiece' by music critics, *Cowboy Carter* came out on 29 March 2024 – act II in the trilogy kicked off by Renaissance.

While some were surprised by her musical choice, it made perfect sense to anyone who had closely followed Beyoncé's career and noted how her influences have included everything from R&B, dance, country, and rap, to zydeco, blues, opera, and gospel. Why wouldn't she explore her country music roots?

'I have favourite artists from every genre you could think about,' Beyoncé reminded the world in her 2024 GQ interview. 'I believe genres are traps that box us in and separate us. I've experienced this for 25 years in the music industry. Black artists, and other artists of colour, have been creating and mastering multiple genres since forever.'

Beyoncé accepts the Innovator Award from Stevie Wonder onstage during the 2024 iHeartRadio Music Awards

Cowboy Carter album artwork

Like *Renaissance* before it, *Cowboy Carter* was similarly conceived during the Covid lockdown. Originally seen as the first of the planned trilogy, Beyoncé changed the order of release, considering that the public needed cheering up with the more glittery, dance-driven electronic vibe of *Renaissance* after the social deprivations of the pandemic.

But now, after five years in the making, the acclaimed album came out to break more records, principally making Beyoncé the first Black woman to top the Top Country Albums chart. Although she said that she felt 'honoured' to have done so, she did voice her hope that, 'years from now, the mention of an artist's race, as it relates to releasing genres of music, will be irrelevant'.

As well as topping Billboard's Hot Country Songs chart, the album's lead single *Texas Hold 'Em* also got to #1 on the all-genre Hot 100.

Comprising a mammoth 27 tracks over 80 minutes, and across a blend of genres, the album was born from an experience where Beyoncé said in an Instagram post, that she had not felt welcomed. 'But, because of that experience, I did a deeper dive into the history of Country music and studied our rich musical archive,' she told her followers. 'It feels good to see how music can unite so many people around the world, while also amplifying the voices of some of the people who have dedicated so much of their lives educating on our musical history.'

Then she signed off by saying, 'This ain't a Country album. This is a "Beyoncé" album'.

The Daily Telegraph described it as '...packed with smart lyrics, astonishing singing, rich harmonies and bold rhythms teasingly inflected with the acoustic guitars, pedal steel and fiddle signifiers of a genre she and her (admittedly extremely large) team of top producers, co-writers and collaborators have ripped apart and put back together in entirely new shapes. Clever, sexy, angry, soulful, witty and fantastically bold, Beyoncé stirs up the western and puts the 'you know what' into country'.

The album cover showed Beyoncé in a red-white-and-blue outfit, high-heeled boots and a sash, holding the American flag while sitting side-saddle on a white horse.

In her 2024 interview with GQ magazine Beyoncé expanded on her inspiration and intentions for *Cowboy Carter*.

'I wanted everyone to take a minute to research the word *cowboy*. History is often told by the victors. And American history? It's been rewritten endlessly. Up to a quarter of all cowboys were Black. These men faced a

world that refused to see them as equal, yet they were the backbone of the cattle industry.

'The cowboy is a symbol of strength and aspiration in America. The cowboy was named after slaves who handled the cows. The word *cowboy* comes from those who were called boys, never given the respect they deserved.'

Aiming to right that wrong Beyoncé gave Black artists, established and new, an opportunity on this album. As well as big-name collaborators such as Willie Nelson, Dolly Parton, Miley Cyrus and Post Malone, were lots of other less well known artists.

The album also featured Linda Martell who broke barriers in country music back in the 1970s by becoming the first Black woman to find commercial success in the genre, with top 40 singles and a solo album.

Beyoncé leaves the Luar fashion show in Brooklyn, New York, 13 February, 2024

Beyoncé and Jay-Z during the 66th GRAMMY Awards, 4 February, 2024

In a similar vein she sampled the half-French, half-Caribbean composer Joseph Bologne, known as Chevalier de Saint-Georges, in her track *Daughter*. Chevalier, the son of a slave, upended racial stereotypes in 18th century Franc and challenged for the top spot at the Paris Opera, yet has little mention in music history as much of his work was destroyed under Napoleon's rule.

Beyoncé referenced his 'Violin Concerto in D Major, Opus 3, No. 1: II. Adagio', created in the 1700s, as a testament to his vision, saying, 'I hope it inspires artists, as well as fans, to dig deeper and learn more about the Black musical innovators who came before us. Some of the most talented artists never achiev the mainstream praise they deserve, especially when they defy the norm'.

Limited edition album cover artwork

Cowboy Carter ▸

Eighth solo album and second in planned trilogy, 29 March 2024

Track listing

Ameriican Requiem
Blackbiiird
16 Carriages
Protector
My Rose
Smoke Hour
Texas Hold 'Em
Bodyguard
Dolly P
Jolene
Daughter
Spaghettii
Alliigator Tears
Smoke Hour II
Just for Fun
II Most Wanted
Levii's Jeans
Flamenco
The Linda Martell Show
Ya Ya
Oh Louisiana
Desert Eagle
Riiverdance
II Hands II Heaven
Tyrant
Sweet * Honey * Buckiir
Amen

Beyoncé's Levi Jeans campaign on the streets of Los Angeles

'This ain't a Country album. This is a "Beyonce" album'

Beyoncé:

Long may she reign

Incredible as they are, sales, awards and accolades aren't the only proof that Beyoncé – Queen Bey – is a force in modern popular culture.

She has impacted almost every aspect of the music industry, from how work is created to how it's released, all the while skilfully defying conventions to explore uncharted territories, establish new standards and pave the way for others to follow. She's adept at reinvention and collaboration and consistently demonstrates an exceptional level of control over her image, music, and business ventures.

Aware that her every move will be analysed, she knows her power and reach and uses it well; her recent albums are as much about the politics of America as music and performance.

Going forward she seems certain to continue her mission to reclaim her heritage on behalf of all. 'I am here to change that old narrative,' she told GQ magazine. 'I've learned that true success is about leaning on a name, it's about crafting something genuine, something that can hold its own. It's not about being perfect, it's about being revolutionary.'

Long may she reign.

Beyoncé speaks during a campaign rally for US Vice President and Democratic presidential candidate Kamal Harris, 25 October, 2024

Beyoncé's voice: A symphony of strength & soul

In her own words...

'Singing is not work for me. I sing for me. I love music and I love to sing. It's a passion that runs deep. There's magic in the way it feels in my throat, a resonance that vibrates through me. When I am at my lowest, when I've been sad or in a heavy fog, sick or anxious with sleepless nights, I sing. And, often, I sing alone.

'My voice has always been my companion. It's why I have always been able to be happy alone. Music understands my heart even when I can't find words. But always, it's in those private sanctuaries – the studio, the car – where I find my peace.

'Singing soothes me, it steadies my heartbeat, it's my best hit of dopamine. There's a certain magic in sitting at the piano, and letting my fingers play random chords as I just let any and everything come out. Singing has healed me time and time again. It's been my refuge.

'It's one of the deepest joys of my life, a necessity as vital as breath.'
As told to GQ in 2024.

What the critics say...

Beyoncé's vocal prowess has been much praised by critics who have variously described her delivery of her songs as **'powerful, versatile, and emotive'.**

As she wraps her voice around complex melodies, with seemingly little effort, she demonstrates remarkable vocal control, even during her physically demanding dance routines. She is famous for using the melisma technique – where a single syllable of text is sung while moving between several different notes in succession – to add emotional intensity and embellishment to her songs. Characterised by intricate runs and powerful delivery, her vocals have been described as both growling and fierce, yet buttery and seductive.

Beyoncé:

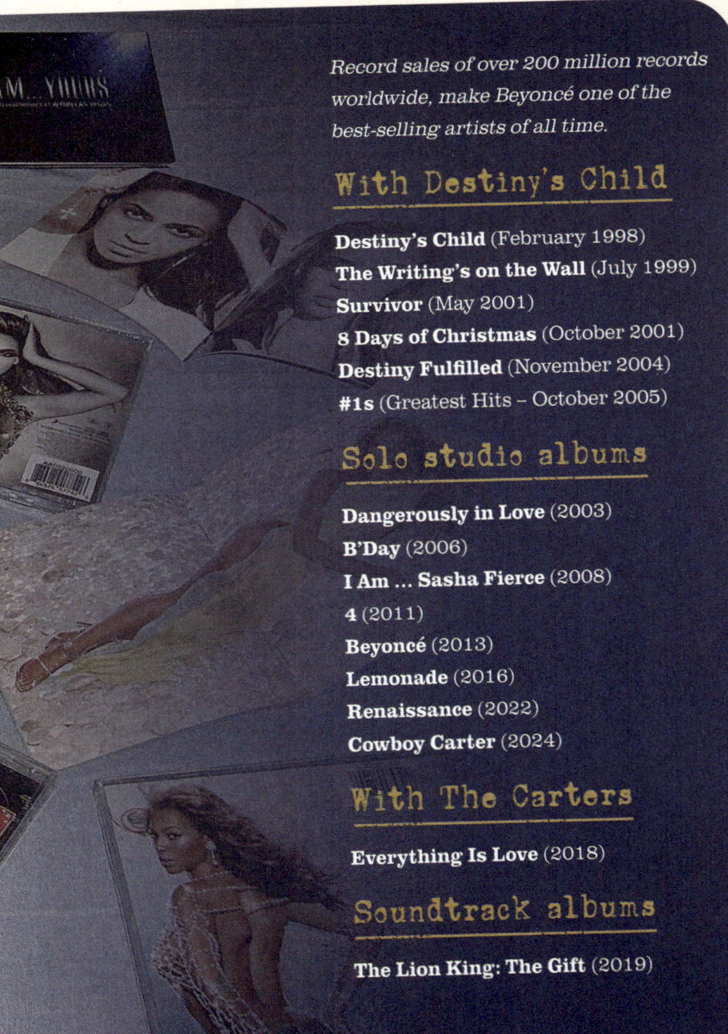

Record sales of over 200 million records worldwide, make Beyoncé one of the best-selling artists of all time.

With Destiny's Child

Destiny's Child (February 1998)
The Writing's on the Wall (July 1999)
Survivor (May 2001)
8 Days of Christmas (October 2001)
Destiny Fulfilled (November 2004)
#1s (Greatest Hits – October 2005)

Solo studio albums

Dangerously in Love (2003)
B'Day (2006)
I Am ... Sasha Fierce (2008)
4 (2011)
Beyoncé (2013)
Lemonade (2016)
Renaissance (2022)
Cowboy Carter (2024)

With The Carters

Everything Is Love (2018)

Soundtrack albums

The Lion King: The Gift (2019)

Discography

Stand out singles

Beyoncé has released over 60 singles as lead artist, 17 singles as a featured artist, 13 promotional singles, and six charity singles. She has sold over 114 million singles in the US alone, with her biggest hits as lead artist including:

Crazy in Love (2003)

This dynamic fusion of pop, R&B, and hip-hop, marked Beyoncé's explosive debut as a solo artist. The standout track from her *Dangerously In Love* album, featuring Jay-Z, the track's infectious horns, commanding vocals, and fiery energy capture the intensity of passionate love. Its banging beat and catchy chorus make it a timeless anthem, solidifying Beyoncé's position as a powerful force in music as she got her first solo #1 on the Billboard Hot 100. It was also the only song that year to top the charts on both sides of the Atlantic when it hit #1 in the UK too and won the 2004 Grammy for Best R&B Song and Best Rap/Sung Collaboration. The chemistry between Beyoncé and Jay-Z was undeniable, and their relationship became a focal point of media attention.

Beyoncé performing a choreography to *Crazy in Love* with her background dancers

Single Ladies (Put a Ring on It) (2008)

Single Ladies (Put a Ring on It) is an empowering celebration of independence and self-worth, challenging traditional relationship dynamics. Beyoncé's assertive lyrics and bold delivery, combined with its infectious beat and hand-clap rhythm worked superbly with the accompanying highly stylised dance routine which became a viral sensation. Its accompanying black and white video had more than 525m views and was nominated for nine awards at the 2009 VMAs. Its failure to win the Best Female Video award sparked the infamous Kanye West incident when he interrupted the actual winner Taylor Swift's acceptance speech to claim Beyoncé had been robbed. She did however triumph with her win that night for overall 'Best Video'. The song was #1 on the Billboard 100 for four weeks as well as topping the charts in the UK, Australia and Canada and generating over six million digital downloads.

If I Were a Boy (2008)

One of the standout tracks from the "I Am..." side of Sasha Fierce, this powerful ballad with stripped-down production and poignant lyrics, explores gender roles and the dynamics of relationships. Beyoncé sings from the perspective of a woman imagining how different her life would be if she were a man, highlighting the double standards that often exist in relationships.

Halo (2009)

Another significant track from *I Am... Sasha Fierce* is *Halo* a soaring ballad that has become one of Beyoncé's signature songs. A declaration of love and admiration, with Beyoncé's vocals shining against a backdrop of ethereal production, *Halo* was a massive hit which highlighted Beyoncé's ability to convey deep emotion through her music.

Run the World (Girls) (2011)

This bold and defiant song, blended elements of Afrobeat drums and percussion with powerful feminist messaging. The lead single from her album *4*, it was a relatively moderate hit (by Queen Bey standards) at #29 in the States and #11 in UK, but a Top 10 hit in other markets, and has had longevity as an enduring anthem for women everywhere.

Love on Top (2011)

This up-tempo R&B song, from the album *4*, was #1 on the US Hot R&B/Hip Hop chart for seven consecutive weeks and won the Grammy for Best Traditional R&B Performance at the 2013 award ceremony. It debuted and peaked at #20 on the Billboard Hot 100 chart, the second highest debut of any of her solo singles at the time.

Formation (2016)

This powerful anthem addressing racial pride and social issues debuted and peaked at #10 on the Billboard Hot 100 and made #3 on the UK singles chart. The song's bold message and iconic Super Bowl performance sparked conversations on Black identity and police brutality, solidifying Beyoncé's influence in both music and activism.

Break My Soul (2022)

The lead track on Renaissance, *Break My Soul* was Beyoncé's first single release from an album in six years. A floor-filler dance track, it featured strongly in the 2022 'Best Songs' lists of all leading publications, won the Grammy for Best Dance/Electronic recording and steadily climbed the charts to become Bey's eighth solo #1 single.

Texas Hold'Em (2024)

The up-tempo, banjo-driven lead single from her country album *Cowboy Carter*, describing a fun night out, Texas-style, the catchy *Texas Hold'Em,* provided Beyonce with the highest solo single debut of her career and best showing of the decade as it galloped into the Billboard chart at #2.

Movies

Carmen: A Hip Hopera (2001)
Austin Powers in Goldmember (2002)
The Fighting Temptations (2003)
Fade to Black (2004)
The Pink Panther (2006)
Dreamgirls (2006)
Cadillac Records (2008)
Obsessed (2009)
Epic (2013)
Lemonade (also director) (2016)
The Lion King (2019)
Black is King (also director) (2020)
Mufasa The Lion King (2024)

Black is King - Beyoncé wears a design by Saudi designer Mohammed Ashi

Documentary and concert films

Live at Wembley (2004)
The Beyoncé Experience Live (2007)
I Am…Yours (2009)
I Am…World Tour (also director) (2010)
Live at Roselad: Elements of 4 (also director) (2011)
Life Is But a Dream (also director) (2013)
Live in Atlantic City (also director) (2013)
On the Run Tour (2014)
Homecoming: A Film by Beyoncé (also director) (2019)
Renaissance: A Film by Beyoncé (also director) (2023)

Beyo